Praise

"A 'Right now!' leadership book."
— **Adele Stickland**, organizational
psychologist, trainer, ICF coach and
1 international best-selling author
of *Get Gorgeous & Accredited*

"This is the leadership model for the digital era."
— **Robin Speculand**, global pioneer
and specialist in strategy and digital
implementation, Thinkers 50 alumnus,
number one international best-selling
author of *World's Best Bank: A strategic guide
to digital transformation*

"If you want to be a growing, dynamic business, then
read this book."
— **Paul Hargreaves**, CEO of Cotswold Fayre
and author of *Forces for Good: Creating a
better world through purpose-driven businesses*

"*Unleash the Inner CEO* provides the rationale and
the blueprint to make leadership at all levels happen
for real. It's practical, well researched and will
help many organizations as they embrace the age
of empowerment."
— **Dan Sodergren**, co-founder, YourFlock.
co.uk, head of diversity at Manchester
Publicity Association, founder of Great
Marketing Works, technology futurist and
AI advocate, BBC TV and News, BBC Radio

UNLEASH THE INNER CEO

Make distributed leadership a reality

JEREMY BLAIN

Re think

This edition published in Great Britain in 2024
by Rethink Press (www.rethinkpress.com)

First edition published under the title *The Inner CEO*
in 2021 by Panoma Press

*To my mum, Carolyn Blain, who has never
had a problem with unleashing her inner CEO.
Thanks for blazing the trail!*

Contents

Foreword

Back in the 1990s, after graduating from business school, I landed my first job at a boutique strategy consulting firm, which turned out to be a crucible of learning about strategic thinking, collaboration and analytical rigor. After successive roles in strategic planning at two different Fortune 500 companies, I started to realize that, despite the cognitive stimulation that came with my work, the best conversations seemed to happen after I left the room. Something was going on – let's call it "leadership" – that seemed to determine whether the strategies my team and I had recommended would work or even move forward toward an execution plan.

After nearly twenty-five years in the learning and leadership development space, I've become ever more curious about not only how leadership happens, but where, and in what circumstances, especially when it comes to aligning whole organizations. More recently, as we approach a post-pandemic reality, we have been given a unique opportunity to reflect on the forced planet-wide experiment on what distributed work can look like, how we can creatively and adaptively solve wholly new problems and how we can unlock the power of collaborative human potential. This has only reinforced the timeliness of this book and the urgency of taking a renewed look at what leadership can do.

The first edition of *Unleash the Inner CEO: Make distributed leadership a reality* positioned leadership – operational and strategic – as something that can be owned by anyone, regardless of level, function, experience or role. This second edition furthers that discussion by going beyond the notion of individual empowerment to embrace the need to shift entire cultures to not only allow for distributed leadership but also nurture it. It is for executive leaders, offering inspiration as to how they can create an organizational culture of experimentation, boldness and trust. It is aimed at human resources (HR) professionals and line managers, guiding them through this culture change with practical, innovative professional development strategies. In addition, it is for individual contributors at all levels, providing the tools to help them unleash their inner CEO and become an "in-role CEO": someone empowered to lead with creativity, innovation and purpose. This second edition also includes stories from those who've had a go at unleashing their inner

CEO and offers caveats and "watch-outs" – times when too much of a good thing can go wrong.

Why is such a transformation urgent and necessary now? For perspective, I work for one of the top leadership education firms in the world. This has allowed me to build a career in developing the mid-to-upper levels of leadership in some of the world's leading businesses across six continents. It has also afforded me the opportunity to talk frequently to the bosses of those leaders. In these C-suite conversations, I normally pose a question or two about their biggest worry regarding leadership in their organizations. Almost universally, especially over the past three years, I've heard some version of the following response:

> "What my team and I need from these leaders is more autonomy and independence in solving the problems that they are closest to. We are simply too far from the action; things are moving too fast and the situation is too complex to expect strategy to be a one-way cascade. We cannot be asked for permission every time we hit a new challenge. We need to provide leaders with clarity on the big questions – purpose, desired outcomes and overall direction – but we cannot be relegated to the role of "approver of last resort". We need them to jump in and act, even if it's uncomfortable. On the flipside, we owe them a lot more clarity on these big questions."

This worry, along with an environment of accelerating complexity, disruption and pace is, I've worked out, a driver behind why "courage" has become so fashionable in leadership circles today. The C-suite wants more courage to act amid ambiguity simply because they need more autonomy to navigate a new, uncertain and fast-changing context.

I've even been asked to try to teach courage, which is, of course, as ridiculous as it sounds. On the other hand, I find it helpful to think of four critical conditions as being necessary for an act to be "courageous".[1]

For an act to be courageous, the person undertaking it must:

1. Experience fear or anxiety associated with the action

2. Genuinely believe that the action will result in negative consequences for them, based upon a rational assessment of the situation

3. Have the perception of a free choice

Allow me to pause here. So far, this represents an act of carelessness. What makes it courageous is the fourth condition, which is that the person undertaking this action must also:

4. Be in pursuit of a supraordinate goal

This last one means that the action must also involve taking a stand for something bigger than oneself.

In *Rehumanizing Leadership: Putting purpose back into business*,[2] my co-author and I explore the importance of purpose, empathy and meaning, not just at an organizational level, but also at a team and individual level, in creating the conditions for alignment, self-direction and sustainability. We found that not only are purpose, values and vision fast becoming the key levers for building clarity and focusing organizational energy broadly, but also that they provide the "guardrails" necessary to help individuals embrace their autonomy to step up to leadership in those moments of truth that call for it.

We live in an age where everyone must live and breathe purpose-based leadership if organizations are to exhibit the autonomy and agility needed to survive. The good news is that we are finally admitting to ourselves, after all the how-to books on the complex task of leadership have been written, that tapping into our underlying humanity – our empathy, values, sense of purpose and desire to contribute to the betterment of other humans – is the best formula for leadership. It has been under our noses the whole time. What's more, we're realizing that this is a *shared* experience. All must feel and act from their own humanity. This, it turns out, is leadership.

Executive leaders need courage to truly unleash leadership at all levels: they must let go of the day to day and trust their people to lead without having to ask for permission. This book calls on middle and senior-level leaders to support a new culture of empowerment in their organizations and it shows how teams can take ownership and experiment, through coaching and a human-centered leadership approach. *Unleash the Inner CEO: Make distributed leadership a reality* will arm leaders and managers with the know-how to make this a reality in their organization, as well as guiding individuals who are ready to step up as unleashed "in-role CEOs".

As it turns out, hierarchy is not necessarily the enemy. Hierarchy can provide clear signposts for career advancement. However, power can lead to decreased empathy in those who wield it and dependency on direction in those who don't. This means that leaders must use their power with greater wisdom and discretion than ever. Far beyond a democratic movement, which is about how power is distributed, shared leadership is about how clarity is distributed. Now more than ever, leaders must use their power to drive shared clarity and inclusion. Jeremy Blain's invitation to unleash our inner CEOs is no less than a rethink about how we can transform organizations into powerhouses of leadership when levels are either absent or meaningless. This will lead to more productive, sustainable and thriving institutions. Ultimately, this book is an exploration of how we can step up without waiting to be asked. It is an invitation to jump in and try it out. Yes, it takes courage, but it will not only be worth it, it will energize and nourish others to do the same.

I hope you accept Jeremy's invitation wholeheartedly and, while you're at it, "forward it to all."

Michael Chavez, global managing director, Duke Corporate Education, October 2023

Preface
To The Second Edition

The scope, scale and pace of change are challenging organizations and executive leaders everywhere. We have not so much entered a new age of distributed leadership as hurtled into it, with all the opportunities and difficulties this brings.

Tapping into the power of the many, rather than the few, by unleashing leadership at all levels and creating what I call "in-role CEOs", drives a more collective and collaborative approach to organizational growth. At the same time, this releases executive leaders, non-executive directors and boards to focus on navigating an increasingly complex, transformational landscape.

In the first edition, *The Inner CEO: Unleashing Leadership at All Levels* I argued that we were entering a new age of empowerment in which distributed leadership, or leadership without levels, can flourish. What struck me during the writing of both the first and now the second edition of this book, is the dearth of manuals, blueprints and how-to playbooks for actually making distributed leadership work throughout our organizations. There have been articles, examples and case studies, but no comprehensive body of work that provides the strategic insight and operational implementation steps to get it right, build momentum and embed the approach culturally by instilling values and behaviors that are bought into across the organization. Yet almost daily we discuss the concept of leadership without levels as the next big thing. We have been talking about empowering others, distributed leadership and more autonomous working for over a century. However, we are still not getting it right.

In the first edition, I set out to provide a corrective: the blueprint to make distributed leadership a reality. I am pleased to say that the book received an overwhelmingly positive response: *The Inner CEO* is now multi-award-winning and a number one best seller in five countries, and across eleven different categories on Amazon.

Since the first edition was published in 2021, I have been working with clients all over the world to implement the distributed leadership blueprint – at both the organizational level and with individual contributors. Along the way, I have uncovered new stories and new ways of explaining concepts and have conducted interviews with more of the people involved.

The challenge, of course, is integrating all of this new information into the existing body of work, and providing even more examples, updated models and guidance for those on the journey to implementing distributed leadership successfully. Enter this second edition, newly updated and enhanced. I have updated previous examples and overall context, with new elements to spark ideas, help problem-solve and ensure successful leadership without levels across our organizations.

The new and improved second edition provides:

- The case for unleashing leaders without levels; it includes a brand-new, up-to-date context for why one leader is not enough, articulated through a new model: The Triple Now©

- Three new ways we can empower people to encourage greater autonomy and psychologically safe distributed leadership: stepping in, stepping out and stepping up

- New interviews looking at empowerment in our businesses, our communities and in structured institutions like the military; Tim Lupinacci, CEO of Baker Donelson, one of the top law firms in the US, adds his insights on distributed leadership at relevant points throughout the book

- Interviews and case studies to highlight the voices of the empowered; these are individual contributors who have unleashed their inner CEO, talking about the ingredients for success and "watch-outs" to guard against failing before we begin

- A brand-new chapter that focuses on how distributed leadership can go wrong and the negative side of empowerment; in the first edition, I talked a lot about the benefits of successful distributed leadership; the second edition balances this with a discussion of the cost of not doing it, or of getting the implementation wrong, and the damage that can be done

- Examples and implementation stories from clients I have been working with over the past three years

Unleash the Inner CEO: Make distributed leadership a reality will arm not only senior executives but also individuals who are ready to grasp the opportunity to unleash their inner CEO, with the why, what and how-to, alongside clear steps to make this a reality in their organization.

STOP PRESS!

We are living and working in the digital age, and I argue that digital tools and working techniques give us a unique opportunity to make distributed leadership the reality we have been talking about for decades. Therefore, it seems perfect for me to practice what I preach and bring this publication into the digital era, beyond merely an ebook.

As such, I am partnering with BlockRank, a Web3 organization, to offer exclusive digital artworks to everyone who is kind enough to buy a copy of my book. Everyone can access their own digital asset for free, and that comes with an additional 5% off any of the associated services I offer through my business, Performance Works International. I will also offer three tiers of rare digital artworks, which come with an investment fee, and grant access to large discounts, free sessions, keynote presentations, and free books for you and your team. You can find all the details and two separate QR access codes to claim your digital artworks at the back of this book following my concluding chapter.

Introduction

From the early days of my career, I have always sought to contribute to the wider team, function and overall business beyond my job description. For example, I would get involved in wider company projects, cross-functional collaboration and more. I noticed that in some organizations, this was easy to do. In others, I was constrained by a traditional management structure that did not encourage or even acknowledge the benefits of truly empowering people.

As I progressed through my career, this kind of empowerment was often referred to as "leadership at any level". More recently, it has been described as "distributed leadership", or "leading without levels", to indicate a flatter structure and more horizontal management. It means a narrowing of the capability gap (especially regarding digital skills) between the top and the rest of the organization. The underlying principle is to harness the leadership potential that exists at all levels to tackle the complex strategic and operational challenges facing most businesses today.

I have called this "unleashing the inner CEO". In other words, it's empowering individual contributors – regardless of level, function, experience or role – to contribute inside or outside of their core job description, both operationally and strategically. The concept of unleashing the inner CEO encapsulates both mindset and action. It is about leadership belief, and about taking ownership to make something happen. It's at the heart of making distributed leadership a reality.

As I evolved into a business leader, learning professional and HR expert, I began to empower and train people to unleash *their* inner CEO. I did this not only with permanent employees but also with an increasingly independent workforce of highly valued collaborators, resulting in more significant mutual benefit, appreciation and loyalty. These can be hard to come by in our fast-changing times, a trend that I explore in more depth in Chapter 1.

I have encouraged this form of leadership without levels across my increasingly blended workforce (permanent and independent workers; office-based and remote) in my own way, with help from experts I respect, without necessarily having a how-to manual.

"Leadership without levels" does not mean that the hierarchy is entirely broken down. We need to protect strategic decision-making and support operational decision-making in different ways. This is especially the case when introducing horizontal management practices, or when faced with the increase of micro-enterprises and DAOs (decentralized autonomous organizations). By definition, these are empowered groups or teams with the autonomy they need, but they must be supported by coaching-centered management and senior leader mentorship.

There are huge opportunities over the next decade and beyond. A "think differently" mindset and transformation agenda have been fast-tracked by reactions to the Covid-19 pandemic, war, resource scarcity, economic uncertainty, the climate crisis and more. These add to the challenges already facing executive leadership, and on-board agendas, such as digital transformation – particularly the rapid rise of artificial intelligences including Claude 2, Chat GPT-4, Bard and many more. We then also need to factor in the rapid shifts in ways of working that we are still embedding. In this context, the need for senior leaders' own development to stay in line with modern-era knowledge, skills and behavior, becomes urgent.

But we have a solution at our fingertips: unleashing the power of the many, rather than the few, as we tackle short-term business needs while protecting long-term prospects. My goal with this book is to guide you on an exciting journey into the emerging world of work and all its possibilities, where you will discover what we can do in the face of continuing, radical transformation. At the heart of successful change is a new approach to strategic and operational leadership. Unleashing the inner CEOs in our organizations is no longer a choice – it's a must-do if we are to build a more collective, engaged approach to strategy implementation and take ownership of critical actions. This approach benefits our business, employees, customers and other stakeholders.

As you read, you will find that the book is written in a practical style to accelerate implementation in the workplace. It's relevant for all sizes of organizations, local, regional or global. I will arm you with precise execution steps, including a 90-Day Road Map, an assessment tool and an action toolkit to give you everything you need for success. This means that you will start in the right way and build momentum as you measure results from day one, which will provide a crucial foundation for the journey ahead. You *must* be successful. Too much is at stake for our organizations and our people as we look ahead to the next five years and beyond.

Here's how our journey will unfold:

- Chapter 1, The New Age, provides context for why distributing leadership is so important, outlining where we stand now and identifying the scope, scale and speed of the transformations driving this change in culture (the Triple Now©).

- Chapter 2, A New Approach For Changing Times, outlines what is meant by unleashing the inner CEO and the underlying concept of distributed leadership.

- Chapter 3, Supercharging Organizational Progress, guides leaders, HR professionals and managers on how they can drive this culture change at an operational level.

- Chapter 4, Making It Happen, covers the steps to be taken toward unleashing the inner CEO at the individual contributor level. It presents a practical, accessible program that will enable individuals to embark on this journey with the support of managers, HR professionals and their colleagues.

- Chapter 5, When Distributed Leadership Goes Wrong, explores the negative side of empowerment. For example, what happens when it takes the form of words rather than actions, and when it fails before it has a chance to become embedded and accelerate?

- Chapter 6, Measuring Employee Empowerment, sets out an empowering approach to measurement. It provides the means for individuals, managers and leaders to track the impact of unleashing the inner CEO, for themselves, their teams and the organization as a whole.

- Finally, the conclusion looks ahead to the challenges and choices of the twenty-first century as we reimagine our organizations. It is a call to action, inviting you to incorporate the models and learnings in this book.

In parallel with creating the framework and training content for this book, I decided to bring the concept of the inner CEO alive by exploring existing best practices and expertise, so the book is full of practical advice, models and actionable steps. I interviewed a variety of business experts, industry leaders, CEOs, talent and human capital professionals, as well as learning leaders from a broad range of businesses. In these interviews, they share their experiences and unique perspectives on the value of unleashing inner CEOs at all levels, and in different businesses. They highlight the ingredients of success and reveal the rapid cultural shifts required to make progress. These interviews complement the theme of each chapter.

In parallel, I interviewed individual contributors at different levels in their organization to pull out their experiences of an empowering culture and of taking ownership with strong support from senior leaders and line managers. Of course, we also bring out in these interviews what doesn't work. Where are the roadblocks to success and what is the impact on individuals if this culture is not implemented consistently, or without momentum and follow-up?

Unleash the Inner CEO: Make distributed leadership a reality fills a gaping hole in the market, and this is the perfect time to unleash the reality of considered and strongly supported distributed leadership. Now is the time for leaders without levels in our organizations, globally, who are encouraged to be more autonomous in their decision-making and their contribution.

In essence, this book is the how-to manual for creating in-role CEOs to unleash the power of the many in these transformational, challenging, unpredictable yet exciting times.

Let's begin.

ONE

The New Age

In this chapter, we'll talk about what leading in an era of unrelenting change means and involves, covering:

- The digital revolution and how it does, and will continue to, impact our lives and businesses

- Increasing opportunities and increasing failure risk – two sides of the same business transformation coin

- The Triple Now© model – providing context to show why one leader is not enough in our organizations

The digital revolution

Industry 4.0, the Fourth Industrial Revolution or the "digital era", represents the coming together of the physical, the biological and the technological for the first time in human history. The velocity and systems impact of this revolution make it distinct from industrial movements of the past. Just consider one aspect of this digital movement: the speed of development and power of artificial intelligence (AI) with, for example, Claude 2, Chat GPT-4 from Microsoft, Bard from Google and Ernie from Baidu in China. We can now look forward to almost limitless possibilities as the pace of digital innovation accelerates. However, we must know how to regulate it, utilize it and manage it, retaining a deeply human touch. That is the magic of digital: to *enable* humans, not to replace or take away from them.

Revolutions bring change, and each of the four main industrial revolutions – the 1784 water and steam mechanical revolution; the 1870 mass production and electrical energy revolution; the third revolution of 1969 with the introduction of IT and electronics; and today, the fourth revolution of cyber-physical systems, ie, the digital age – has changed the world. As we look back, we can see that each caused widespread, heavy casualties for businesses that did not respond to their changing environment. Corporations that are unable, or unwilling, to adapt to the new waves of innovation coming their way are marked for certain failure.

We've witnessed a stream of well-known brands fading to obscurity when management teams failed to adapt. Gary Vaynerchuk said of Kodak and Toys R Us, "They did not innovate, and when you do not innovate you die."[3] More recently, high-profile legacy and new-era businesses have suffered the same fate, by not taking lessons from the past and making the same mistakes. JC Penney and Bed, Bath and Beyond could have invested more in their digital platforms to offer gold standard out-of-store, online offerings.[4] This, coupled with a charm offensive to win over customers, could have paid dividends. Alas, there was too little, too late.

New-breed digital platform businesses are not immune to these mistakes, and it is perhaps these that offer the biggest lessons of all. The below examples[5] show that constant evolution, a razor-sharp competitive edge, customer understanding and buy-in to the proposition, are all now essential.

- Hipmunk – a travel aggregation platform since 2010, did not continue to innovate and was surpassed by existing and emerging platforms, such as Expedia, Skyscanner, Trivago and more.

- Atrium – a legal industry start-up aiming to shake up a traditional industry. Its failure was driven by complexity and sunk costs, demonstrating how difficult it was to be a major disruptor in traditional industries, with complex underlying systems and regulations to navigate.

- Quibi – perhaps one of the most notable digital-era failures, despite a US$1.75bn investment fund, much excitement and hitting a hot button (short and longer-form video content and streaming for mobile devices). When considering what went wrong and just how much investment could have been squandered so quickly, the conclusion is simple. What could go wrong, did go wrong. That points to a huge leadership failure on a human level and is a warning shot that other digital businesses should take heed of.

Today, leaders must adjust, realign and build a new mentality and approach to digital business model transformation and human-centered leadership in their organizations. The challenge – or opportunity – can be far bigger than many (even experienced) senior leaders can imagine or are capable of dealing with. They need help, particularly in this new, digitally driven, fast-paced business environment that we are all a part of.

A call to action is needed to unleash the potential of distributed leadership, to allow the power of the many to flourish and contribute beyond the expectations of their level of seniority or job description. As the capability gap between the most senior leaders and the rest of the organization narrows, particularly when we consider digital-era knowledge, skillsets and behaviors, we have the prospect of tapping into the combined resources of the many. Not just the few or the one at the top. This is the opportunity we must grasp to deal with the (sometimes overwhelming) transformational context we face.

This chapter brings all this together and sets out the context in a new model: the Triple Now©. This model is designed to help executive leaders, managers and individual contributors understand the scope, scale and speed of these strategic transformations and operational changes that they face, which require the careful involvement of all personnel. Navigating these changes effectively will be for the benefit of all: customers, stakeholders, employees, executive boards and the senior leadership.

The Triple Now ©

The fast pace at which we live and work today is driving both incremental and radical change in business and is becoming the new normal. Some organizations are keeping up, but many are being left behind. It is no longer a question of when or whether it's a good idea to transform organizations in preparation for the future; it is now an urgent question of *how* to transform.

In the current workplaces and beyond, we will experience dramatic shifts as we encounter a perfect storm of forces that will challenge our companies, leaders, managers and teams on a worldwide scale. These three forces – the Triple Now© – will serve to either propel or block the success of businesses in this transformational era.

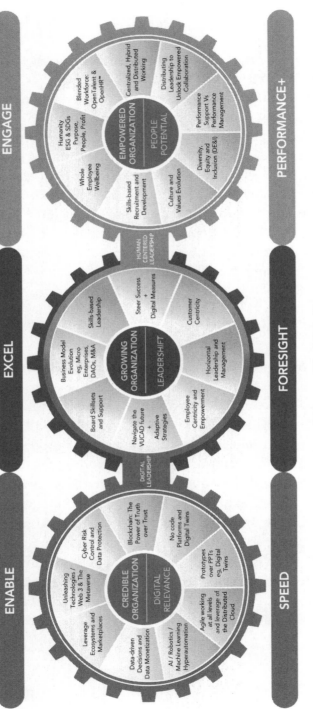

Figure 1: *The Triple Now*

The Triple Now: The journey to digital relevance

The first of the three forces is digital relevance. A digital transformation is needed to harness the power of the digital revolution. To facilitate this change, a mentality shift is essential, at the leadership level and throughout the organization. The most successful

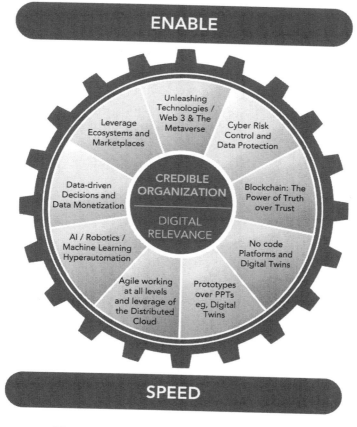

Figure 2: *The Triple Now – Digital relevance*

organizations are making strides and undergoing fundamental change, whereas others who are unwilling to change are already falling behind, or failing.

There is a lot to reflect upon, for many legacy and new-era businesses. We need to prioritize and understand what the "future-now" landscape looks like. To do that, we must consider the various aspects of the current digital revolution that we need to spotlight and master, across the business and at all levels.

AI and robotics are pivotal and will soon be everywhere. In 2023, with the launch of open AI systems like Chat GPT-4, many businesses were, for the first time, beginning to understand the potential of AI in the workplace. It is important, though, to consider the risks of not having a structured regulatory framework in place to act as a fail-safe where required.

It is a fact that AI will be used by everyone and be in everything that we use, from a lifestyle as well as a business perspective. AI will become more intelligent and efficient because the technology that drives it is rapidly developing (for example, hyper-fast bandwidth technology, Web 3 and 6G-9G mobile networks).

Furthermore, as blockchains, cryptocurrencies and NFTs (non-fungible tokens) give power back to users in the form of ownership, we will be witness to a new game-changing digital combination that will drive innovation and a surge in new products, services and solutions. This will unlock the power of digital transformation, to the benefit of customers, companies and employees.[6]

These technologies and others will inherently shift more and more of what we do to the cloud, rather than taking place in/on physical spaces or devices. That's why Microsoft transformed from a computing company to a cloud company, as did Amazon, moving away from digitally enabled retail. The Amazon cloud is one of the most used systems of its kind out there for large organizations, particularly for those changing their business model to be ready for the new digital era.

These technologies will also help realize the potential of concepts such as smart cities, immersive gaming, autonomous vehicles, personal AI and robotic assistants, the Internet of Things (IoT) and more. They will be applied to solve problems and find solutions to our current challenges, such as climate change, availability of resources, commodity scarcity, fossil fuel reliance, population growth, mass migration, war, economic models and much more. All this will have the military-grade security of blockchain and the ease of use of your favorite app.

That said, as with any new progress leap or technology, we have to be aware of the risks and narratives associated with innovations. For example, we are in the infancy of AI's development and there will be things to watch out for and unknowns to navigate. To avoid being too starry-eyed, we should all take time to read about, learn about, experiment with and then apply new digital technologies and tools in ways that benefit the organization, its customers and its employees.

The current era is bringing together the digital with the human touch. Some call it the phygital age – the coming together of the physical, biological and digital. Leaders at all levels must have the ability to select and apply the appropriate technology to fit the purpose and use it to enable a high-touch way forward, enabling those accompanying them on the journey to collaborate, share and communicate effectively and efficiently. *How* we operate in the digital era is critical. Technology and the human touch are inseparable – one won't work without the other. Cooperation and communication are required to build small, empowered, self-owned teams that manage themselves and are supported by technology, not overwhelmed by it.

I would urge readers to take a look at all seven aspects within the digital relevance component of the Triple Now© and consider my questions related to each:

- **Unleashing technologies, Web3 or the Metaverse.** How much do you know about these? What kinds of innovation, perhaps that you haven't even considered yet, might they unlock?

- **Cybercrime** is one of the most proliferate industries in the world – you *will* be hacked. What are you doing about that now? How can you use blockchain to give you military-grade security and an additional platform for innovation?

- How will these digital components **unlock new digital value** within your organization and how can you tap into that in the short term, for the benefit of your customers, employees and business?

- Digital transformation is not just about technology. It's about adopting **new ways of working**, such as Agile methodology, at all levels. How are you changing the way everyone, including senior leaders, works in the organization to be faster, more efficient and more empowering?

- How can generative **AI, machine learning and robotics** support your business strategy and operations going forward, to unlock the potential of hyper-automation and human-centered design?

- What new roles and skillsets are required at all levels to enable better quality **data management**, from data input to data output; from data spreadsheets to data visualization; from data mining to data-based decision-making and monetization?

- Are you still investing in individual systems and platforms? How much progress have you made in creating **digital ecosystems**? Ecosystems are the gateway to seamless connection, where different technologies talk to each other and better enable your business, providing a more stable opportunity to build and add marketplaces as extensions of your customer offers.

The risks of neglecting the digital component

Most organizations, as you may imagine, aren't ready to tackle this monumental shift to and within digital. For example, let's take just one component of our digital wheel: cyber risk. According to a blog by EliteGroup, if cybercrime was a nation-state it would be comparable to the third largest GDP in the world.[7] The companies that grasp what going digital means, and how to be digitally secure – protecting employee and customer trust – will gain a competitive advantage. Digital acceleration will also accelerate the need to regulate, manage and control cyber risk and the impact of cybercrime.

Understanding is a crucial feature of getting the digital component right. For many, it is a huge task to comprehend all of the dimensions within the digital component of the Triple Now and then navigate action, at speed. It requires a dramatic mentality shift, and this has to happen at the executive leadership and management levels first. From my research, I've found a lack of understanding at senior levels in the organization to be the biggest blocker of progress in this area. Almost half of all leaders surveyed did not have a vision for the digital era, and 40% of those had no intention of developing one.[8] This affects everyone else in the organization and is a route to rapid failure, not long-term success.

I am interested in how technology and digital ways of working can supercharge businesses and people everywhere. Autonomous, empowered work can become the norm and leadership of ideas, actions and growth can happen at all levels of our organizations. This can be supported by lighter hierarchies and managed horizontally to unleash the potential of the many, rather than the one executive leader who feels they need to have all the answers.

All of us, regardless of level, need to understand the immediate digital world influencing our lives and our work. The digital component of the Triple Now brings this into sharp focus. Many of us have a lot to learn to understand how it can enable a more human-centered focus in our ways of working. Once we achieve that, we are likely to be working more efficiently, more productively and more collaboratively with others. The digital component is, therefore, the key to unlocking the next part of the Triple Now – the human component.

The Triple Now: Unleashing people potential

This second force is relevant to any transformation, business model evolution, bricks-and-mortar policies, appropriate human capital frameworks and the embedding of new ways of working like hybrid and distributed. It represents almost as big of a workforce transformation as the digital component. What's more, it's one that not all senior executives and board members know enough about. More worryingly, in my experience, many HR professionals are also not as aware or skilled in how to unleash people potential as they should be – so how can they credibly advise and help the executive leadership group in this area?

This is both urgent and important. The human shift, not unlike the digital shift, is challenging businesses everywhere and is a highly involved process.

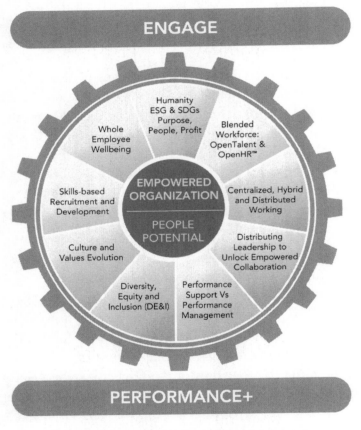

Figure 3: *The Triple Now – People potential*

As we consider the human component, I'll highlight some of the most important aspects that organizations need to consider, plan for and become proficient at. One of the biggest transformations is the rise of the blended workforce. This is not about simply hybrid working; it relates to the increasing mix of permanent employees and independent workers, alongside the many other ways in which people now identify themselves in the world of work. There are digital natives and non-natives, remote workers, transnational digital nomads, virtual assistants and contingent workers.

As leaders, we need to consider whether we will continue to hire a predominantly permanent human resource. Will we move to a "flexible worker first" recruitment model? Or will we utilize an equitable recruitment policy for both permanent and independent workers, as part of our modern employee ecosystem? The latter is becoming the preferred workforce mix for many organizations. Beyond managed services and ad hoc project work, OpenHR™ experts have predicted that by the end of the 2020s, many workforces globally will be made up of 50% independent workers and contractors, and 50% permanent/permanent part-time workers.[9] Leaders will need to formalize the new blended workforce model and integrate independent specialists, workers and longer-term contractors into organizations as part of the human capital ecosystem alongside permanent workers.

There is currently no human capital framework that fits this model, although more work is being done in this area, notably by Open Talent solutions expert, John Winsor, and Dr Rochelle Haynes and myself (on the OpenHR™ model). John Winsor sums up well the "miss" on this workforce transformation trend: "The war for talent is over – and talent won."[10]

A new human capital framework is required to lead and manage this integration effectively, as part of overall organizational culture-building, collaboration, recognition, communication and reward systems. We will also need to ensure that the first component of the Triple Now, digital, underpins our workforce mix evolution, and the different workplaces, spaces and models of working that are now in place. Technology is now everywhere and unavoidable and is a huge enabler for a transformational organization and a more flexible, empowered workforce. The Organization for Economic Co-operation and Development (OECD) projects that nearly one-third of all global jobs, amounting to over a billion, will undergo technological transformation in the 2020s.[11] As technology continues to mold our personal and professional spheres, there's a pressing need for a wider, more varied and skilled workforce to take on the challenge and lead our tech-centric businesses and innovations into the future.

For example, how will we employ AI to provide consistent and controlled data access to everyone in the organization, regardless of designation, location and job role? How might AI facilitate highly effective collaborative working? And how can AI enable truly autonomous, empowered working, without levels, across all employees, both permanent workers and the formalized independent mix of workers?

Our people – regardless of who they are, where they are and how they are engaged – must be encouraged to embrace the digital tools and new ways of working, to take ownership of what they're doing and collaborate with their peers, seniors, subordinates, customers and partners to an extent they never have before. Organizations need a strong commitment to enhanced learning and development journeys to build digital-era priority competences, regardless of role or level, and in turn, raise the capability bench and provide a gateway for the broader organization to get involved in strategic and operational plays. This will truly unleash the potential of the many, and further reinforce the case for a bold new age of empowerment across the organization.

Culture building

Culture building will be at the heart of any human-centered transformation. When we put digital transformation together with the workforce and human shifts, we must consider, in parallel, an expansive culture-building strategy. We have to think about the values and behaviors that will underpin the evolution of the organizational culture so that everyone can thrive in this new era.

A thriving culture for the digital era is adaptable and responsive to the vast opportunities, as well as the formidable threats and challenges, presented by technology, the disruption of markets, changing customer behaviors, the evolving workforce mix and changing ways of working. Ultimately, it is achieving the correct blend of the digital and the human that will be paramount to achieving the necessary cultural shift.

An inspiring example of an organization that has successfully facilitated this shift is DBS Bank in Southeast Asia, which has been repeatedly recognized by the Euromoney Awards as the best digital bank in the world. Its CEO, Piyush Gupta, said, "If you want to compete, you must embrace the digital and the human together, and then build the new culture around that."[12]

Fundamental to the bank's success has been its ability to take risks and its willingness to experiment to understand what works and what doesn't, while maintaining its focus on the customer. The organization appears to be obsessed with continuous change and data-driven decision-making, which is paying off. DBS is an excellent example of what happens when a company seizes the opportunity of digital transformation; when the leadership mindset and actions align with transformational needs; and when the whole workforce is engaged, mobilized and owns part of the shift. This is transformational leadership without levels.

Ultimately, the most important criteria for success are first, to understand that you're on a technological voyage, and second, that this understanding is reflected in a significant cultural shift in your organization. You simply cannot separate the digital from the necessary human journey. It is by engaging with the forces of digital transformation and leadership readiness (the third component of the Triple Now) that the big culture shift required for the digital era becomes possible. By achieving the culture shift, the hierarchy is flattened and the rest of the people in the organization are supported and encouraged to unleash their inner CEO.

As far as the blended workforce goes, this is also being embraced by companies like Your FLOCK – a scale-up in Manchester, UK – which is anchoring independent, flexible and permanent employee recruitment and retention strategy squarely within organizational culture and fit. It firmly believes that getting the right hire can provide stability, performance and longevity for all parties, avoiding a potential culture clash.[13] It has since extended its app-based solution to define, check and enhance team cultures as a key component of organizational success and people engagement for the Triple Now era.

As with the digital component, I urge you to consider a few key questions across the different aspects of the people potential component:

- Employees and prospective employees are increasingly looking at the role their organizations and leaders play beyond the corporate walls. These leaders need to be more **humanity-centered and purpose-driven and to value people in different ways, balanced with the need to make money.** How is your organization progressing in getting this balance right? How important do you think it will be in the future?

- How are the **blended workforce and new work models** affecting your business? How fast are you creating new human capital frameworks to support a blended workforce? How are these shifts impacting the customer and employee experience you are striving for?

- What is the mindset internally to truly **distributed leadership**? What structures and processes need to be updated to support the move? How important will a more empowered workforce be for fueling faster innovation and growth?

- What are you doing to overhaul your **performance management** systems? How can senior leaders and line managers become more coaching-centered, with strong on-the-job support and a growth mindset?

- What **diversity, equity, inclusion and accessibility** measures are important to your employees, stakeholders and customers? Are you moving the dial in inclusivity terms? Are you creating a psychologically safe environment to supercharge diversity of thinking, fair inclusion and a sense of belonging across the organization?

- Are you communicating and adopting the **values** and behaviors, at all levels, that will lead to an evolution of "**good culture**" in the business?

- What are the existing **knowledge areas, skills and behaviors** that need an upgrade? What are the new knowledge areas, skills and behaviors that will prepare your organization and workforce for the future? How can you hire and develop your people from a skills-based lens as you evolve as an organization, and as new requirements arise that may not have been visible before?

- How will you protect the mental and physical **wellbeing** of all your employees, regardless of designation, level or role, as human beings? How will this impact culture building across the organization?

As final food for thought around the human transformation piece, we return to the connection to digital transformation that is accelerating in parallel. With the unleashing technologies and the rise of generative AI, we must also consider what I describe as "warm versus cold", which is the human worker working alongside the artificial or robot worker. This will become a real situation for many, as smart technologies and intelligences are increasingly integrated as part of the workforce, not just the workplace.

The Triple Now: The Leader*shift*

The third and final component of the Triple Now is all about how boards and senior executive leaders are readying themselves to navigate the future while steering short-term success. For many, this has been, in part, an acknowledgment of the need to embrace a steep learning curve regarding many other aspects across the Triple Now. For others, this will simply be a matter of survival or failure. The scope and scale of the transformational space are overwhelming and are affecting mental health and physical wellbeing. This raises the fundamental question of how to cope in these fast-moving, unpredictable and unnerving times.

Figure 4: *The Triple Now - Leadershift*

It can take an equal dose of vulnerability and courage. The vulnerability to acknowledge what leaders do and don't know. The courage to embark on a new learning journey; to ask for help; and to unleash the power of the many in the organization, as digital-era skillsets narrow the capability gap between the very top and every other level in the business. Leaders may not be the smartest people in the room anymore (if they were ever), and that requires a mindset shift for some legacy leaders who favor more traditional, hierarchical leadership expectations and practices. As an example, here's the first of our insights from Tim Lupinacci, who has been at the forefront of Baker Donelson's transformation:

> "We have as a company gone through a lot of change management – particularly our mindset shift in trying to think of ourselves as a business, rather than a law practice. It's not always easy, and there is trial and learning with everyone involved. With this mindset, we have been building broader expectations and accountabilities beyond other law firms and our partnership consulting know-how. This is about gaining a competitive edge, it's about being agile, and about not being complacent."

As you reflect on all the points within the central leadershift component, consider the journey senior leaders and managers need to go on, to fuel ambitions across the digital and people components of the Triple Now:

- When did you last challenge your existing **business model**? How will it need to adapt or fundamentally change to protect your business's future? And how will the business model itself fit into the digital and people components of the Triple Now?

- Just as it is with the workforce, the need for **skills-based leadership** is now urgent and important. The sheer pace of change, and the need to transform organizations everywhere, are challenging leaders in new ways. New knowledge, skills and behaviors must be adopted. That starts with a mindset shift.

- Defining strategies is what many leaders have proved they are good at. However, **implementing strategy** is something different entirely. More than 60% of strategies are still failing,[14] not because of poor strategizing, but poor implementation, planning and execution. The leadership question has firmly shifted from "what" we need to do, to "how" we execute successfully, with everyone being a part of the journey.

- To unleash the inner CEO across the workforce, it may be that legacy **management structures** (largely vertical hierarchies) need a rethink. What progress are you making in challenging the current system? What, if anything, needs to change?

- One of the main reasons why a horizontal management structure (detailed further in the next chapter) is more suited to today's workplace is the strong foundation it provides for greater **employee-centricity and unlocking a new age of empowerment** in all organizations. This is what will make distributed leadership a reality and multiply growth efforts internally, for the benefit of customers and other stakeholders externally.

- A fundamental question I ask all C-suite leaders I meet is: Who are your executive board advisers and are they competent across each dimension of the Triple Now? In other words, do they have the capability to advise and provide the kind of governance that is required in a Triple Now-era organization? From my own experience of serving on several boards, I have been shocked at the lack of understanding of the modern workplace by some senior advisers. In particular, this concerns the transformational landscape across both the digital and human components of the Triple Now, and the need for **greater support for C-suite leaders** who may require help and more current and correct advice. Without it, risk management and governance at the board level could be a huge issue.

A leader's role is to navigate the journey to long-term success, at the same time as protecting the short-term opportunities, risks, challenges and unpredictability that are increasingly a part of modern business. It's a lot to take on, particularly when considering the digital and human transformations of the Triple Now. The sheer scope, scale and speed of transformation can be overwhelming. It demands thinking through new business models, new ways of working, less traditional management structures and a new relationship with employees at all levels.

Greater autonomy and distributed leadership – allowing the workforce to make more decisions in their role, as part of the team and more strategically – can ease the burden on senior executives. In turn, they can focus on navigating the complex future many anticipate, while short-term operational execution and success are driven and owned across the business, without traditional levels. There is still a need for a hierarchy, but it can be repurposed to act as a performance support, rather than a performance management function.

We are all in it together, and those businesses and leaders who understand that; who balance purpose, people and profit; who transform digitally and understand the importance of the human component, are those who are most successful, as we will see below.

Companies that are getting it right

In the digital era, speed of progress is more important than size or legacy. There is no longer such a thing as "too big to fail" or "too famous to fail". It's more likely that you'll be too slow to succeed. Jessica Tan, co-CEO at Ping An Insurance says:

"I worry about not being fast enough... There are just so many things to do, and speed is of the essence. What's especially exciting about China is that you may be the best now, but if you're not fast enough, a 70% solution can beat you."[15]

The Chinese company Ping An is a great example of an organization that is transforming from a traditional banking and insurance company to a leader in insurtech and fintech. This embracing of the possibilities provided by digital adoption is enabling internal and external services, solutions, collaborations and partnerships that are driving consistently high-quality customer experiences far beyond any of their competition.

Ping An has the mentality that a 70% solution can beat you if they get there first. The need for speed means that in the digital world, we are becoming more accepting of experimentation, and even failure. We don't necessarily need the perfect solution we strived for in the twentieth century. We need something we can build on and improve in rapidly evolving versions, like our apps, software and personal devices. Technology glitches and patches are part of our daily lives. Why should that not apply to innovation in business across our products and services? When managed correctly and communicated effectively, experimentation can be hugely beneficial and drive competitive advantage almost overnight.

Take Chat GPT-4 and Claude 2. Open AIs are imperfect beasts, but Chat GPT seemingly came out of nowhere and was rapidly updated to Chat GPT-4 as an early gamechanger. There were glitches to start with, including false data and accusations of plagiarism. However, the speed at which this technology has evolved has been astonishing.[16] It has left Google's early development of Bard lagging (evident in the share price within hours of Chat GPT's launch)[17] and China's AI developments (Ernie by Baidu) also some way behind. As Tan claims, speed was the key. The speed of a 70% solution established a first-mover advantage and AI dominance for Microsoft. For now.

Technology is everywhere and unavoidable, so every job in every company is being or will be changed by the digital revolution. The largest traditional non-tech companies have found ways to transform and thrive, realizing significant, previously unseen benefits of adopting digital and innovating in spaces that had been closed to them. For example, Nestlé, Adidas, Unum Group, Nike Kweichow Moutai, DBS Bank, Raffles Quay Asset Management and many, many more.

With this kind of transformational digital fire-power, organizations everywhere can find a new way to structure themselves, operate and transform for the modern era. A big part of this will be tapping into the human-centered component of business and unleashing the potential of the many. By "the many", I mean leaders at all levels who are willing to step out of their job role to contribute strategically as much as operationally. Their time is now, and the time for those organizations and senior executive leaders who can't or won't change is running out.

What next?

So where to start? It feels like a huge task. We are trying to transform our organizations, embrace the digital revolution and unleash the power of our people, all at the same time. However, there are success stories out there. What follows is the first of seven main interviews that accompany this book. These interviews bring in external thought leadership, existing best practices and examples of organizations getting it right (and wrong). These interviews, together with the recommendations and models I provide in this book, give you a blueprint that will help you to accelerate progress, taking into account learnings from those who have gone before and new and emerging practices.

Our first interviewee, Johanna Bolin Tingvall from Spotify, would argue that the threshold of the digital era, our new industrial movement, is precisely the place where great things can happen, including unleashing the empowerment and support of in-role CEOs.

Interview with Johanna Bolin Tingvall

Johanna Bolin Tingvall is currently the global head of learning and development at Spotify, based in Stockholm, Sweden. Johanna has been at the forefront of HR and learning throughout her career and leads human capital development through GreenHouse, Spotify's internal learning and development function.

In this interview, Johanna explains how the development of built-in strategies for unleashing creativity and cross-business collaboration is enabling Spotify to innovate faster than its competitors. In this way, Spotify is unleashing the human component of the Triple Now©, enabled by its digital environment.

JEREMY: As we head into the 2020s and beyond, how important is it to restructure, remove layers of hierarchy and empower people so that leadership at all levels is unleashed?

JOHANNA: With the ongoing development of technology, the world is moving much faster, and decisions are being taken at a speed never heard of before. Things change quickly, which means it is increasingly difficult to make decisions in the traditional bureaucratic way: with hierarchies and levels of management. It's just too slow. All levels need to be involved in decision-making. It's simply more efficient and productive – and more engaging.

Another consideration is innovation and how the pace of innovation is driven. You need to unleash the power of everyone's ability to come up with great ideas, much quicker and more efficiently than in the past.

JEREMY: If I can relate it to Spotify, a digital-era business, how does this level of empowerment benefit the company and the individuals stepping up and taking ownership?

JOHANNA: Based on research, we know that autonomy – particularly having the ability to make our own decisions – is a strong motivator, and we see it every day. We have built-in ways of working for letting creativity loose.

For example, in our regular "hack weeks" we empower everyone to work together and focus on whatever they want. They can innovate anything. A few of our greatest ideas for new Spotify solutions, such as Discover Weekly, which is a weekly mixtape of recommended music tailored to each listener, have come out of this.

This creates a high level of engaged employees, and diverse creative solutions being created and implemented quickly. These are big benefits for any company getting it right.

JEREMY: How does this support career pathing if we use a traditional approach? Or does it drive something different?

JOHANNA: We don't have traditional career ladders because they don't work in Spotify's fast-changing environment. Instead, we talk about growth.

Someone who starts working with us may not get a new title or a promotion every six months, but they will have the opportunity to learn and grow. The job will not stay the same because it will constantly shift, change and throw up new challenges and opportunities to handle. You grow yourself and, in turn, help to grow the company. We strongly believe in a growth mindset.

JEREMY: From your experience, what conditions have to be in place at C-level – culturally and structurally – to enable people to safely and successfully unleash their inner CEO?

JOHANNA: The conditions have to be driven from the top. Spotify is by culture a rather flat company, but still, we have our CEO, Daniel Ek, who has set the scene here. We're a purpose-led company. Every member of the team knows where we're going and why, and we have a strong set of values to guide the way, enabling a transparent company climate that builds trust. Of course, the culture will evolve with each new person who joins the company.

JEREMY: How does this manifest itself in terms of how it feels to work and be a contributor at all levels at Spotify?

JOHANNA: It clarifies direction for the company and how we can all contribute inside and outside our job roles. I also think the flat hierarchy we have at Spotify is important. We don't have the typical bureaucracy where if you have an idea, you have to go to your manager, then it has to go to the next level of managers. With us, if you feel your idea is strong enough, you can go straight to Daniel.

JEREMY: So if we're creating an empowering culture built on the DNA you've described, which has until now mainly been for permanent employees, is this the same for the independent workforce? And how would that work?

JOHANNA: We discuss that a lot at Spotify. When it comes to the way you do your job or your level of autonomy, we don't make a distinction between our permanent and non-permanent resources. We're a transparent company and anyone who comes in, whether a contractor or a permanent employee, has access to practically all information through our internal communication channels. It's hugely empowering, engaging and motivating for our workforce, whether they are permanent or independent workers.

JEREMY: When we look at the hard facts, does this drive as much mutual value between Spotify and its independent contractors, as it does with permanent employees?

JOHANNA: Yes, I see it work every day, but there are some differences. We may have a contractor filling an interim role for one year or someone coming in to deliver just one training session. So, of course, it differs. Overall, value is most effectively derived from our permanent resource, but there is strong value in the independent resources we use, and they are treated with respect and openness.

JEREMY: It's been fascinating talking with you, Johanna, and I have just one more question. What is the cost for those companies that resist transforming into a modern, flatter organization that truly empowers people?

JOHANNA: I believe the cost will be high if they can't find new ways of increasing innovation, engagement and speed within their companies. They will have a hard time attracting the talent they need, and they will most likely be left behind when it comes to innovation – meaning they will struggle to keep up with the competition.

We need some structure and a support network, but not too much. Over-control destroys creativity and innovation. At Spotify, we live in controlled chaos. We have the structure in place to avoid total chaos, but it's in the chaos that unexpected new, great things happen. That's where innovation often comes from.

TWO

A New Approach
For Changing Times

In this chapter, we will cover:

- Some definitions of key terms stepping in, stepping out, stepping up: the three ways to empower your workforce

- The Five-Point Star: a model for identifying future leaders at all levels

- The principles and benefits of horizontal management: creating flatter organizations

Unleashing the inner CEO within our organizations can create the competitive advantage that is now essential in our changing times. In this chapter, I set out the concept of the inner CEO and the keys to unleashing it. It is relevant, therefore, for all audiences:

executive leaders seeking to understand the strategic possibilities offered by unleashing CEOs, HR and organizational design, and individual contributors. What follows is the essential how-to for identifying those ready to unleash their inner CEO, and what is needed to empower them for their journey.

Throughout this chapter and beyond, I bring in the voice of the empowered as a bridge between what we envision a truly empowered workforce can be and what it looks like in reality, with early lessons from individual contributors who have been empowered successfully and, at times, not so successfully. My thanks to Rasie Bamigbade, Milvio DiBartolomeo and Ehecatl Hunt-Duarte for their time and feedback.

Who or what is the inner CEO?

What I mean by "the inner CEO" is that potential within individual contributors at any level to innovate, generate ideas and lead a plan into action, going beyond the boundaries of their "role", but without having to stop and ask for permission.

The ability to collaborate with all levels, as well as with peer groups, results in an increased degree of effectiveness and productivity. In this new era, people must not only be excellent at their individual job roles but also make a strategic contribution to the business.

Who are in-role CEOs?

In-role CEOs are those who have realized this potential, having unleashed their inner CEO. They are empowered to lead operationally and/or strategically, beyond their core role. Unleashing inner CEOs, whatever their level, to become in-role CEOs, will herald a truly empowered workforce, backed by repurposed, supportive management lines and a leadership team that moves away from a reliance on "command and control" and into a state of enablement.

Who is responsible for unleashing the inner CEO?

Executive leaders, HR professionals and managers, as well as individual contributors themselves all have a role to play in realizing this potential. Executive leaders do so by creating a culture of empowerment and trust while being strongly supported by their board. HR professionals and managers can implement this culture and facilitate the development of individuals seeking to unleash their inner CEOs.

And of course, individual contributors play their part by taking responsibility and being accountable for successful implementation while being strongly supported by management along the way.

Stepping in, stepping out and stepping up

Making distributed leadership work depends greatly on your people's preferences, stretch and personal development path. It's easy to misdirect and be inconsistent across the organization, which is why there is a strong need to create the conditions for empowered, autonomous work to thrive. This must be driven by the executive board and leadership team and reinforced by repurposed line management approaches throughout the business. This is all discussed in chapters three and four, with the how-to tools to make it happen.

Once the conditions have been created, the next step is empowering individuals in the right way. This is about working smarter, more autonomously and more productively, with strong alignment to organizational, team and individual goals. Empowerment is not always about doing more, extra or incremental activity on top of the "day job". This is an important myth to dispel early in conversations. Empowerment can sometimes drive incremental effort but is more often about working smarter, activating a personal development journey, and business growth.

Each person should own their empowered role in the organization with the support of management, rather than always being supervised. This makes all the difference, as it also creates the basis for a true coaching culture across the organization: a line management that is more focused on performance support rather than almost wholly on performance management.

This is something I will repeatedly call for within this book, as it enables a much more glued-together, collaborative workforce, which transcends traditional levels, layers, perceptions and expectations.

There are three "right" ways to empower the workforce – ie, ways suited to the organization and the individuals unleashing their inner CEO. These represent three stages of empowerment, from taking ownership within a job role to more strategic contribution and involvement. The stages do not necessarily represent a linear journey but provide a platform for internal planning, discussion and involvement with the broader organization from day one. Individual contributors should be supported by their line management to find the right stage for them, based on personal preference as to where they feel they can best contribute. As in-role CEO Ehecatl Hunt-Duarte, public sector employee, describes:

> "It was important that I wasn't just getting dropped in at the deep end. I was able to explore more breadth. In previous roles, I knew people who were dropped in at the deep end and they eventually left. I was able to say yes to things when I felt ready to take them on – there was a psychological safety net in place."

There is certainly an evolved "will" and "skill" component to work through collaboratively.

- **Stage 1: Stepping in** – Enhanced contribution in the job role and with other team members

- **Stage 2: Stepping out** – Working across the broader function or on cross-functional collaboration initiatives, projects and tasks

- **Stage 3: Stepping up** – Contributing beyond a specific job role, function, level and/or country, both strategically and operationally

I will explain what each of the above stages means in turn, with suggestions of activities that empowered individuals can take ownership of. I will also talk about how leaders and management should support the movement by embracing horizontal management practices, a growth mindset underpinned by a strong coaching culture and a focus on performance *support* over performance *supervision*.

Stage 1: Stepping in

An individual's leadership can be enhanced within their current role without necessarily going beyond the boundaries of their job description or team. This means being more productive and efficient every day. It's about being unleashed to make decisions without going to a manager, problem-solving independently and/or with others, ideas generation, team plays and implementation and new ways of collaborating.

"Stepping in is a great way to get people to do more work." This is our first myth to bust. Stepping in means greater autonomy within a specific role, enhancing that role. This will also benefit and often involve other team members. What follows are suggestions of things that line managers and individual contributors can discuss together. This is not an exhaustive list but a starting point for a more collaborative initial conversation and a tailored way forward for everyone involved – add your own ideas and actions.

Many of these ideas, we could argue, are implied in a job description. However, often only the minimum is done, or we get caught up with admin, unproductive tasks and other people's agendas. Stepping in helps us seize the initiative and own our job role and how we execute day to day.

Ideas for those stepping in to the job role with other team members:

- Take ownership beyond the day to day within the role. For example, "How can I make my customers' lives better?" (either internal or external).

- Think through ideas that would make the job more fulfilling.

- Set a daily challenge – how to delight one customer, one colleague and one other person today.

- What problems need to be solved? Work out how to lead the solution and involve others or the line manager as required.

- Put yourself in others' shoes and consider how to improve service delivery and build personal and team reputation.

- Set a team challenge to innovate, problem-solve, ideate, drive a special project, conduct a special event internally or externally, etc.

- Rethink team working practices – for example, what best practices are emerging? Driven by the team with line manager coaching support where required.

- Lead team projects, meetings and tasks on a rotational team leader basis.

- Double-up/support others in the team with their tasks, projects and must-dos.

- Own the onboarding effort for new hires into the team, to support line management efforts.

Ideas for management enabling support and recognition of those stepping in:

- Offer coaching support with regular reviews and regular open feedback (both ways). This is a perfect opportunity to provide recognition for the behaviors, successes and improvements that have been observed.

- Set up peer coaching circles within the team as an ongoing support system.

- Enable ideas and discussions outside of the team as required.

- Build skills on the job and corporate activity to enable greater empowerment, autonomy and self-leadership beyond the team job descriptions.

The first of our empowered in-role CEOs, Ehecatl Hunt-Duarte, describes how stepping *in* can deliver excellence and innovation when supported by the right environment and culture:

> "Knowing that my employer trusts me to deliver with little micromanaging gives me a reason to do the best job I can and encourages colleagues to reach out more often when unsure about something. It's also been important for me that my ideas are taken seriously – and that they could get taken forward."

Stage 2: Stepping out

The best operational performers and most experienced team members may not have ambitions to move up the organization or on to other jobs, but they could still have the knowledge, skills and will to contribute beyond their team. This offers a new engagement play and great fulfillment for the individual, reinforcing their worth to the company, the function and the team.

Increasingly, the need to formalize cross-functional, cross-regional and more diverse project groups offers a great opportunity for individuals and even teams to step out of their day-to-day roles.

Stepping out allows for greater internal community building, which is fundamental in bolstering culture and also the values and behaviors suited to a truly empowering organization.

Ideas for those stepping out to the broader function, or on cross-functional collaboration initiatives, projects and tasks relevant to the operational efficiency of the organization:

- Share within the function to adopt best practices and embed new ways of working across the broader group.

- Job share/job swap within the function to provide different perspectives or applications to appropriate challenges and opportunities.

- Design special functional projects to evolve function operations or to enhance service delivery, communication, collaboration, etc.

- Bring in operational expertise at all levels with cross-functional task groups to work on improving collaboration, communication and efficiency.

- Attend cross-functional trade shows or community work outside the business.

- Enable greater efficiency across multiple functions within the business through cross-functional problem-solving.

- Innovate, support and implement new ways of working, through cross-functional projects, bringing in empowered team members from multiple functions. These would be closely supported by management sponsors as coaches, team mentors or sounding boards.

- Support talent initiatives inside and outside the business, especially to excite the next generation of talent about the business, and thinking about careers, placements or internships.

- Reflect new ways of working through collaborative skills building across teams and functions. This will help to build the organizational bench on co-working, project, task and digital communication tools (eg, Teams, Meet, Zoom, Slack, Notion, Trello), leading to greater speed of interaction and more consistent digital competency building across the organization.

- Re-skill experienced members of the team who perhaps will not be promoted but are contributing. For example, providing them with digital working skills, leadership skills for contributing more effectively both within the function and cross-functionally. This could help to prepare them for special secondment projects as part of a cross-functional team or as an individual with management support.

- Use experienced members of the team and high-performers as cross-functional peer coaches or part of learning and development efforts internally. This would be co-owned by employees, strongly supported by HR and learning and development teams.

Ideas for management enabling support and recognition of those stepping out:

- Offer coaching support with relevant team members and with other personnel within the business. This will provide a regular open feedback arena and the opportunity for formalized recognition of an individual's new behaviors and impacts.

- Set up a support system of formal line support and informal mentoring for special project teams, within the function or cross-functionally. This provides a safe space to share concerns, requests for help and so on.

- Create a line manager network for open sharing, representative of all personnel involved in special projects and tasks, both inside the function and cross-functionally.

- Build skills on the job and corporate activity to enable greater leadership skillsets, empowerment, autonomy and decision-making.

Milvio DiBartolomeo, our next empowered contributor, reflects that those stepping out will need to have access to relevant professional development opportunities, which can foster new networks across the organization, and skills development for others:

"People are given professional development opportunities as part of career success planning to improve their leadership skills. There is a network of other leaders and mentoring programs to help people be the best version of themselves, particularly as a leader. I also have access to my line manager and other peers, where required."

Stage 3: Stepping up

Those with the potential for a greater stretch – for example, identified future executive leaders – can be involved in special projects that require something extra. They might attend senior management meetings and contribute more strategically to the business. This stretch must be balanced so as not to jeopardize deliverables in their core role. This may involve incremental effort or activity and is closely aligned to the longer-term development aims of the individual and their contribution to the organization, as much as empowering the individual in the short term.

This may not be for everyone, but in the spirit of distributed leadership and a true age of empowerment, people will have the right and choice to stretch themselves beyond their job role. It is most likely high performance will most comfortably sit in this group, however, as they are on top of their operational role, delivering results and demonstrating a desire to go beyond the role, function and discipline.

Stepping up allows individuals to demonstrate their broader competence, attitude and capability to other functions, across to other line managers and up the line to leadership level – through to the executive C-suite. They need to be strongly supported and sponsored as important future talent to retain and maintain engagement with.

Ideas for those stepping up to contribute beyond a specific job role, function, level and/or country, both strategically and operationally:

- Become involved in functional line management meetings – either to present or contribute in some way – as part of an ongoing working group, as appropriate.

- Exposure to C-suite leadership: present at a meeting, attend part of a meeting, work with an individual leader as part of a functional or cross-functional project, etc.

- Reverse mentoring: bring a high-performing individual (eg, with great digital working competence) into the management team and executive leadership meetings to offer informal developmental support up the line.

- Take part in more strategic meetings to understand the forward plans of the business and contribute from the ground up, feeding into the final strategy definition.

- Be part of a working group with managers, leaders and other individual contributors to own strategy implementation in terms of planning, actions, communication and collaboration within and outside specific functional expertise.

- Cross-regional, cross-functional or country secondments for special project work, or to experience other working practices and to take back learnings into their specific function, team and role.

- Be part of customer engagement or implementation teams, regardless of role, to build understanding of customer experiences and the entire customer journey, and to bring the customer to the heart of the business (again, regardless of function and role).

- Work with HR on career days or as part of potential hire interviews, sponsored work placements or temporary job shadowing.

- Lead external/community projects sponsored by the business, to demonstrate the importance of "giving back" and to be at the heart of a purpose-driven business. This allows for bold leadership (with internal support and sponsorship) external to the organization.

Ideas for strong management support and recognition of those stepping up:

- Offer management coaching support within and outside the function to provide different but aligned management voices. This is useful for broader perspective building, working with different styles, flexibility of approach and more.

- Offer leadership mentoring – usually and most usefully outside of the function, subject to the role and competence level of the individual, having an executive leadership team mentor would be beneficial.

- Fast-track strategic and operational skills building aligned with leadership and management competencies, in parallel with enhanced job role know-how.

- Facilitate regular senior HR discussions with the individual to build a profile of ongoing needs, wants, progress and assistance required, and to officially recognize successes (with both qualitative and quantitative evidence).

Our empowered contributor Rasie Bamigbade, founder of RB Jumpstart Coaching, explains what stepping up looks like in terms of engagement and leadership of the wider team:

> "Listening, meeting everyone in the organiza-
> tion in team meetings or training sessions and
> being inclusive when making changes and
> decisions that affect everyone (surveys/polls to
> get everyone's input and decide from there)."

The Five Point Star: Step in, step out or step up?

For an individual contributor, some key questions will undoubtedly arise. Am I going to embrace leadership at my level? How can I grow in the role? How can I become a leader? What's in it for me? Do I really want this? Where am I most comfortable when working more autonomously?

For executive leaders, HR professionals and line managers, the question becomes: How do we help people identify and embrace their preferences for greater autonomy and support, through encouraging them to step in, step out or step up?

Not everyone will want to step up. Some may step out; some will step further into their role. However, in the spirit of this book, everyone has the potential and opportunity to redefine their job role and break out of a rigid job description, particularly if empowerment leads to greater skills-based working. In other words, this is about utilizing the talent within the organization where it is best placed, without being limited by a formal job description. This is extremely freeing and empowering. Tim Lupinacci suggests what this might look like:

> "For example, some of our non-graduate managers may know what they're doing in areas that they didn't teach in law school. They also might be more digitally savvy than our senior partners. So it's important no one, regardless of

71

level, thinks they are the smartest in the room because of their rank or their degree or experience. We are in this together and we must behave that way."

To make the process more efficient, doing some groundwork can ensure everyone has a say and can appreciate what being empowered means, and the expectations and freedoms that come with it. This is a collaborative discussion, not a formal assessment (which would fly in the face of the idea of buying into the potential in everyone). A two-way discussion of an individual's will, their current knowledge, skills and behavior, and where they feel they can best contribute outside of their job description, is far more likely to result in them feeling fulfilled, engaged and valued.

My Five-Point Star, shown below, is the foundation from which to unleash in-role CEOs. It provides clarity as to the high-level qualities that can be shown by the workforce, at all levels. Again, let me stress that *everyone* has the potential to unleash their inner CEO, and anyone can be invited – but the reality is that not everyone will want to, or succeed if they do. From an HR perspective, this collaborative validation discussion becomes a psychologically safe way to initiate the process and find an agreeable way forward. Everyone is a part of the process and has a choice, and no one gets left behind.

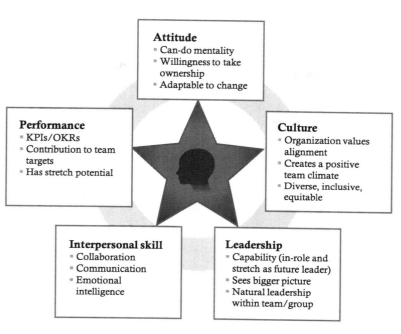

Figure 5: *The Five-Point Star model*

The Five-Point Star model facilitates a collaborative discussion with any individual, at any level in the organization, with their line manager, functional leader or HR business partner. It will help all involved understand and agree on the current status of the individual concerned and the most suitable path forward for them to embrace greater autonomy, as part of a wider distributed leadership and ownership play. The discussion will unfold around the five dimensions of the Five-Point Star model:

1. **Attitude:** What you're looking for is a can-do mentality, willingness to take ownership and adaptability to change. How does the individual feel about this? What is the line manager's view and, if required, how can HR support the process in a positive, empowering way?

2. **Culture:** What are the organization's values, and is this person aligned with them? What is the team culture and how does this person fit into it? What are the enablers and barriers in place within the current culture, and do they need to be modified? And how does the management climate in the organization facilitate truly unleashing and empowering people, according to the individual and their line manager?

3. **Leadership:** This relates to capability. Are individuals demonstrating leadership capabilities in their role right now? This is about the stretch to be a future leader for the business or the ability to evolve within a current role and grow with it. It also concerns the capacity to see the bigger picture; the ability to demonstrate natural leadership in the team and group; and the stretch that has been demonstrated to date – according to both the individual and the line manager.

    In parallel, human-centered leadership traits will be a critical aspect of in-role CEOs, regardless of whether they are stepping in, out or up. These traits might be demonstrated in how the individual currently considers, interacts with and supports their peers, subordinates and those more senior to themselves; in their natural empathy and emotional intelligence; and in their ability to consider others ahead of or alongside themselves.

4. **Interpersonal skills:** Alongside the deeper, emotionally intelligent human-centered leadership traits listed above are the always-important core skillsets of collaboration, communication and other so-called "soft" skills. I would call these power skills, as there is nothing soft about them – particularly when we consider the context of the modern business world. These skills are at the heart of digital ways of working, the blended workforce and hybrid models.

5. **Performance:** Is the individual demonstrating that they can perform at a high level in the team, within their job role and as part of a high-performing organization? Referring back to appraisals and personal development planning and ownership offers a solid basis for collaborative discussion around these points. It is easy to identify those individuals who have shown consistently high performance in KPI terms, who own their development

and who are active contributors to the team
and organization.

Together, these five points form the basis of an
empowering initial discussion that also sends a clear
message of leaders and line managers "walking the
talk". The Five-Point Star can also be used as a quantitative measure for individual self-assessment and
peer and line management feedback. If this sounds
like a preferred route for your organization, the simple 1 to 5 rating system below for all parties can be
used to indicate the extent to which each aspect is
being demonstrated (with 1 being the lowest end of
the scale and 5 being exemplary). The total score will
indicate whether the individual concerned should
step in, out or up.

This simple template (and the examples that follow) will support ongoing discussions with anyone in
the organization and define the most appropriate next
steps, through strong mutual agreement and commitment. This is valuable because, according to Valène
Jouany, "Employees who feel their voice is heard are
4.6 times more likely to feel empowered to perform
their best work. Giving them a voice and a platform
is a giant leap forward in terms of empowerment and
job satisfaction."[18]

In parallel with these empowering discussions,
thought will need to be given to the (re)structuring of

Trait	Aspects to consider	1 = Not at all 5 = Role model	Total
Attitude	▪ A can-do mentality ▪ Willing to take ownership ▪ Adaptable to change		
Culture	▪ Organization values alignment ▪ Creates a positive team climate ▪ Diverse, inclusive, equitable		
Leadership	▪ Capability (in-role and stretch as future leader) ▪ Sees bigger picture ▪ Natural leadership within team/group		
Interpersonal skill	▪ Collaboration ▪ Communication ▪ Emotional intelligence		
Performance	▪ KPIs/OKRs ▪ Contribution to team targets ▪ Has stretch potential		

Rating guideline
45–60 indication: Step up | 30–44 indication: Step out
0–29 indication: Step in

Figure 6: *Five-Point Star assessment template*

the organization as a bold enabler of empowering distributed leadership or ownership at all levels. This then facilitates an individual stepping in, out or up. One of the major benefits of this organizational approach to empowerment is that it provides psychological safety.

Psychological safety

Dr Amy Edmondson, the Harvard professor and scholar who coined the term "psychological safety",[19] described this concept as, "a belief that one will not be punished or humiliated for speaking up with ideas, questions, concerns or mistakes."

Timothy Clark later provided a framework of four stages of psychological safety: inclusion, learner, contributor and challenger.[20] The foundation of "inclusion safety", of respect and validation, is essential – this must be in place before a leader even starts to think about enabling and empowering in-role CEOs.

This closely supports the stepping in, stepping out and stepping up framework. A culture of inclusion takes in-role CEOs all the way through the learner and the contributor stage to the point where they can challenge safely, as part of a culture of experimentation, trust and boldness that leaders must establish.

There must be psychological safety before you can unleash in-role CEOs to thrive and inspire others, at both an operational and strategic level.

The three stages of stepping in, stepping out and stepping up must be supported and enabled by a flatter structure that equips line managers and executive leaders to support individuals. A horizontal management structure enables an authentic effort to boost empowerment across the business, without reliance on traditional layers and levels. Rasie Bamigbade, in-role CEO says:

> "Flexibility, growth and room to coach/contribute to everyone's growth and fullest potential: these were all essential for me to be able to step up. Feeding my ambition, growing in my role and into other roles, leading teams through new projects/challenges, support from other leaders and reaching the planned results: these were all essential to my success."

Horizontal management principles and benefits

As we move toward the 2030s, horizontal management is a rapidly growing trend. Also known as "flat" management, it emphasizes an organization's structure with fewer middle managerial layers, fostering a more inclusive, adaptable and team-oriented environment. This approach seeks to enhance efficiency and communication and to empower everyone in the organization. It moves from performance management toward performance support and is a more collective and collaborative approach to handling the multiple challenges and opportunities that arise in modern business when moving at speed. It is as much a fundamental cultural shift as structural change and will rely on culture-building activity in parallel with implementing flatter management principles.

If we are to unleash a bold age of empowerment that everyone can buy into, that may (for some) mean ripping up the twentieth-century ways of doing things and creating a more agile organization for digitally fueled, accelerating twenty-first-century leadership. I predict that by the 2030s, this will be more closely supported by intelligent AI. Recognizing the evolving workforce transformation and ways of working, our employees will continue to narrow the capability gap between the top of the organization and individual contributors, in terms of the new knowledge, skills and behaviors needed for the digital business era. These are areas that some legacy executive leaders and boards are woefully behind on, or at least struggling with. In fact, they are entering into one of the steepest learning curves across the business, to build their modern business and leadership capabilities and, in some cases, just to keep their head above the water.

With a more empowered, competent workforce, this takes pressure off even the most traditional leaders. They are released to focus on more strategic considerations, as greater ownership of strategic implementation is spread across the business, with the many contributing to enhanced organizational success, rather than the few.

The top ten benefits of a horizontal management structural approach are:

1. **Empowered decision-making.** Rather than a strict top–down approach, team members have more control over decisions related to their

responsibilities and projects. This facilitates swift actions and agile problem-solving.

2. **Trust and empowerment.** Trusting team members with decision-making fosters a sense of ownership, often leading to heightened creativity and job satisfaction.

3. **Transparency in communication.** This creates a culture where everyone feels comfortable sharing insights, critiques and suggestions without repercussions.

4. **Team collaboration.** Absence of stringent hierarchies fosters multi-disciplinary collaboration, bringing in varied expertise and viewpoints.

5. **Minimal red tape.** A condensed managerial structure results in faster approvals, without the unnecessary sign-off layers that many organizations have to deal with.

6. **Adaptability.** With fewer bureaucratic procedures, flat organizations can swiftly adjust to business shifts.

7. **Ongoing skill development.** In a flat structure, employees often juggle multiple roles, emphasizing the need for continuous learning and skill enhancement.

8. **Peer feedback.** While formal assessments might persist, there's a greater focus on continuous feedback from peers.

9. **Accountability and autonomy.** More freedom also means more responsibility. Employees are trusted to innovate but are held responsible for outcomes.

10. **Guiding leadership.** Instead of authoritative roles, leaders in flat organizations act more as mentors or enablers, ensuring teams have the necessary resources and clearing potential roadblocks.

Despite its advantages, horizontal management isn't free from challenges and there are some traps to avoid in implementing horizontal management principles. As companies expand, sustaining a wholly flat framework might get complicated. There can be ambiguity in roles and possible conflicts without an evident hierarchical mediator, as well as inefficiency risks. To address this, some companies opt for a "semi-flat" structure, keeping a middle ground.

Ultimately, to effectively transition to horizontal management, a company must nurture a cultural shift, be open to modifications and utilize strong communication tools to boost teamwork.

Bringing it all together

Applying the learnings from this chapter, we're aiming for an empowering distributed leadership approach underpinned by flatter management and working structures. From decision-making autonomy to job fulfillment to the creation of more creative personal growth journeys, a distributed leadership approach provides a far more supportive, aligned and collaborative environment for everyone to work in.

This approach has been exemplified by Spotify, as detailed in the earlier interview with Johanna Bolin Tingvall. Below are some more examples of companies making significant strides in empowering their employees and realizing the benefits of a distributed leadership environment, while embracing increasingly horizontal management practices. I go into more detail on each of these examples and the empowerment strategies they have adopted during my workshops, but here are the headlines:

- **Google (Alphabet Inc):** Google's famed "20% time" policy lets employees allocate a fifth of their time to personal, passion-driven projects. Numerous Google innovations, including Gmail, have emerged from this. Additionally, the company champions open dialogue, flatter management structures, team synergy and a congenial workspace.[21]

- **Zappos:** Zappos has enthusiastically adopted "holacracy", a self-governance model that decentralizes authority. This approach allows teams to formulate strategies and decisions independently, without routinely seeking a managerial green light. There are downsides to this approach, but it is encouraging to see organizations experimenting like this, with everyone involved.[22]

- **SEMCO Partners:** Under Ricardo Semler's guidance, SEMCO transformed its operational ethos. Employees enjoy flexible work timings, participate in selecting their supervisors and even have a say in their compensation. They're also encouraged to customize their work environments. In some ways, SEMCO excels at leadership without levels. This is not to say there is no hierarchy – there is, but it is light touch until required. This creates a supportive and motivational environment for individual contributors to thrive in, strongly supported by line managers who are constantly improving themselves to add more value to employees within and outside of their function. As a result, traditional functional verticals start to simplify, with greater horizontal value added.[23]

These trailblazing companies demonstrate the potential of an empowered workforce underpinned by an appropriate, flatter leadership and management structure. They show that when employees are vested with trust and authority, they can drive innovation, foster a positive culture and significantly contribute to organizational success. Ehecatl Hunt-Duarte reinforces this idea:

> "It's also been important for me that my ideas are taken seriously – and that they could get taken forward… There's something about having autonomy over your time. This encouraged

me to try and automate some processes, as well as look into different platforms that can be used."

The proof is out there, and it is in some ways a work in progress. Distributed leadership, horizontal management and a truly empowered workforce require a spirit of experimentation alongside the specific guidelines within this book. We are in an era of transformation.

All efforts should focus on and involve the many, not the few. How do *we* work together as a high-performing team? How do *we* focus on our goal to successfully implement the plan? It's about everyone in the team giving and asking for help where appropriate. In-role CEOs must model the desired behaviors and skills and be prepared to support those who are on the journey with them.

How to make it happen

What needs to be in place to enable and empower individual contributors to unleash their inner CEOs, and realize their potential as in-role CEOs? There are three key factors for robust identification and support of candidates who are ready to embrace the opportunity to become an in-role CEO:

- The Five-Point Star collaborative discussions to identify those stepping in, stepping out and stepping up, as detailed earlier in this chapter

- An empowering organization and management structure, supported by updated and creative in-role CEO recognition and reward mechanics, both of which I describe in the next chapter

- A 90-day fast-start, measurable road map and development planner for those unleashing their inner CEO (Chapter 4)

Throughout this chapter, I have stressed the need for a collaborative approach across the business in bringing in a new era of empowered, autonomous working. Making distributed leadership the reality we want it to be requires all parts of the business to come together. This includes executive leadership mindset and sponsorship, reimagining traditional management structures and engaging our leaders at all levels in new ways.

This is not about doing more. It is about being smarter in how we work, more trusting of our people to be autonomous workers, as much as team players; and repurposing leadership and management of others to supercharge distributed leadership efforts, for the benefit of customers, employees and the business as a whole.

What next?

The right environment can be an accelerator of success and help to build the culture needed for the new organizational era. In Chapter 3, I will focus on leadership and culture – the organizational perspective – and Chapter 4 will map out the operational and personal steps for in-role CEOs and their line managers to follow. First, my conversation with Natasha Prasad from Mambu shows how an empowered and distributed approach to leadership can not only further enhance competitive edge, but also provide psychological safety. Natasha details the need to create the right, safe environments for potential in-role CEOs to thrive, and how they should be developed and nurtured by the organization.

Interview with Natasha Prasad

Natasha Prasad is currently head of capability and customer experience at fintech company Mambu, which operates a cloud platform for banking and lending businesses. Throughout her career in sales, service, human capital management and capability roles, Natasha has been passionate about empowering others and providing them with a platform to perform and contribute beyond their core role.

JEREMY: Why is driving leadership through the organization – unleashing the inner CEO – important for today's businesses?

NATASHA: These days, employees are looking to be empowered and recognized for their ability to achieve more, by accessing their broader knowledge, passions and skills to contribute above and beyond their job role. To have a vibrant workforce, organizations must attract and keep the right talent, as well as allow people to take on leadership activities, whether self-based, team-based or task-based leadership.

JEREMY: In terms of actually making it happen, what does the leadership and management mindset need to be, to drive actions to unleash and support inner CEOs?

NATASHA: From a leadership perspective, a growth mindset is critical, as this means having leaders who make it OK for you to test, learn, grow, develop and contribute in bigger, bolder ways. When people feel safe, and when leaders trust their people, this nurtures a healthy exchange of ideas and collaboration. It's about knowing you won't be punished for having a go but will be supported and able to learn from your experiences.

When this starts at the top with the leaders embodying this spirit, it speeds up the process and enables others to do the same and to be supported. Everybody contributes, and everyone grows.

JEREMY: What happens when this doesn't work; when there isn't a safe environment to own leadership at all levels?

NATASHA: A good example of this is what happened with a high-performing colleague in an organization where I worked. She was incredibly smart and such a good operator, but she was surrounded by a couple of alpha males who were out for the glory, and it was their team who would help them realize their dreams and bonuses, rather than the other way around.

My colleague felt bullied and there were no psychological safety protocols to allow her to share her ideas, volunteer to lead tasks or contribute beyond her job role. Any attempt to do so was seen as a threat by her bosses, rather than an opportunity to unleash her inner CEO.

It's such a shame because I have seen this happen so many times, across many different businesses with leaders who think it's a sign of weakness not to be at the front. They are blinkered, so they miss the people in their team with the potential to be and do more. The net impact is that these people will typically look for other roles if they think that they're not appreciated and it isn't a safe environment for them to spread their wings.

JEREMY: It's harder to convince many "traditional" business leaders of the need for a flatter structure, empowered people and a new approach to how we manage. What do we need to do to support their journey?

NATASHA: I'm trying to solve this problem for myself because it is a challenge that human capital professionals encounter. They need to provide these leaders with support on the "what": what leadership at all levels looks like, what a supporting executive body and line management need to do to reinforce and embody it, and what needs to happen to create an evidenced, safe environment for people to embrace the concept and to step up. We must get it right at executive leader level first for it to work across the rest of the organization because otherwise, it will fail.

JEREMY: The obvious follow-up question for me is: what is it like in the companies that do get it right?

NATASHA: In those companies, you see and hear people articulating how much they love working for their organization because they genuinely feel valued and can make a difference. They become brand ambassadors for life, even if they leave. This speaks volumes for the brand in the marketplace. It attracts talent to come and work for the company, and they have a better chance of keeping them after their first motivated and energized ninety days, which is traditionally when commitment drops off.

JEREMY: What are the benefits for senior managers?

NATASHA: Senior managers are freed up to do what they were hired to do: to focus on the strategic direction of the business, anticipate market shift, clear roadblocks, build networks and connections, and ensure that the foundations are in place for consistent levels of winning strategy execution.

I see a lot of leaders being too operational, which is driven by a lack of trust in their teams. They sit there giving orders, and then as soon as their people start to have a go, they criticize and control them.

Senior leaders who are more courageous, who acknowledge and recognize that there are plenty of people with the right attitude and skills to step up, and who can loosen the reins, empower others and accept there will be some experimentation, will realize the benefits almost immediately.

JEREMY: How do we catch people doing it right, driving the proper recognition and reward, on top of what they're getting paid for in their role?

NATASHA: When I've had outstanding leaders in the past, they've been brilliant at positive public recognition and constructive private recognition. They would catch people doing it right in front of others, and also help them with private coaching when they needed assistance or developmental feedback.

There are so many things we can do to keep inner CEOs energized, motivated and recognized. It's a combination of the line manager and senior sponsors, and the culture of the organization and how they do things. Pay increases and bonuses, team recognition, development opportunities and secondments, for example. The less obvious thing is curating interesting experiences for them, whether it's a mental challenge, project task or team challenge that is strongly aligned with their target or is focused on a skillset they're trying to develop.

JEREMY: What is your experience of an organization that does encourage leadership at all levels for people to unleash their inner CEOs?

NATASHA: In one company, I organized a workshop specifically for people we had identified to step up and contribute more to the business, beyond their job role. The intention was to get them to articulate what their future world could look like if they were more empowered and supported to be and do more. They created their future role, defined what success looked like and captured it all in a vision for their future selves. From the vision, I encouraged them to design their objectives and measurables by creating dashboards that would clearly record progress and highlight possible next steps and actions. After this, they all presented their ideas to the executive leadership team. This was a crucial step. The best participants were then sponsored to execute their plans immediately. What followed engaged everyone in the organization. People said, "We can do this, and they will support us."

THREE

Supercharging Organizational Progress

In this chapter, which is about creating the right conditions to unleash inner CEOs, we'll cover:

- The mindset shift required at the top of our organizations

- Considerations for executive boards and non-executive directors (NEDs) – governance in the age of distributed leadership

- How to embed the change culturally across the organization – ie, the organizational conditions required for success

- Line management implications and "must-dos"

- How to re-engineer recognition and reward in line with distributed leadership ambitions

The inner CEO – a strategic and operational balance

Unleashing the inner CEO is about people moving from being almost entirely operational, driven by their job description and KPIs, to becoming more strategic. It is about people stepping in, stepping out or stepping up, as we covered in Chapter 2; about people expanding what they can do, and how they do it, both by themselves and with others across the team. This shift to a more strategic mindset enhances the importance of individual contributors to the team, their function and the company as a whole. No longer are they simply focusing on basic, often transactional job role tasks and must-dos, without an eye on the bigger picture.

But to make this shift, they will need to be supported by a flatter organization with more involved and supportive leadership and management, which potentially affects both strategic and operational levers. This trend is already evident – over the past five years, organizations have been seeking ways to get more from their employees. They have been downsizing, and more pressure is being applied on individuals to step up and beyond their operational roles. There is also evidence to suggest that unleashing inner CEOs has occurred by accident, as a lever to drive performance and grow the organization at a time of fundamental shift and transformation. That said, it has not always been formalized, supported or recognized in KPI and reward terms.

In an article published in *Personnel Today* back in September 2016 arguing for the importance of having leaders at all levels, Dr Tim Sparkes wrote:

> "There's a growing sense that people are itching to lead irrespective of whether it comes with a traditional leadership name tag... The workplace is shapeshifting too rapidly for people to sit patiently and earn their stripes."[24]

Sparkes' article reinforces the shift away from a traditional hierarchical structure. If we consider the Gen Z mindset (the latest generation to enter the workplace), they're ready for this. Based on my experience, they are poised to take on responsibility and use their initiative. Organizations haven't been attracting enough of the right people because they haven't been systematic in their approach. The full potential of the next generation of leaders is, as yet, untapped and unrealized. Therefore, there is a need for an appreciation of the strategic side of things and of the conditions needed for distributed leadership or ownership to flourish, reinforcing a strong movement toward the bold empowerment of everyone.

This is first and foremost the duty of care of the board, executive leaders and line management. Without their alignment, words and actions start to diverge, and the risk is of failure before anything gets started. This then affects the organization and how people engage with a relaunched version of it – they will probably be more skeptical, perhaps even less trusting than before. To mitigate these risks, strong governance and support from the executive board are as important as the commitment from senior leaders and management.

Governance in the age of distributed leadership

The results of implementing the material in this book will support the kinds of rapid organizational transformation we have begun to witness. A more collective and collaborative mindset in leadership terms means that you will have empowered, unleashed in-role CEOs on the ground, delivering beyond their job description. It is, therefore, imperative that organizational governance evolves in line with and to support this.

Executive boards and NEDs

Distributed leadership naturally results in executive boards and senior leaders having the time to focus on the megatrends and the big growth strategies driving what the organization delivers to employees, customers, shareholders and other stakeholders in the medium and long term. These organizations will be ready to adapt to sudden changes, big technological leaps and the continuing integration of digital into how we live, play, work and do business.

But there is a "watch out". These "new" boards and executive leaders will need to select close advisers, including NEDs and strategic consultants, with care. One of the core purposes of NEDs is to contribute toward strategy and ongoing governance, based on their broad and varied experience. However, NEDs whose careers have largely unfolded in more traditional environments may struggle to contribute to future strategy if they lack experience in digital transformation, new working models, flatter management structures and culture building in new breeds of empowered organizations.

The current business landscape demands speed, as the rate of change accelerates in line with ever-newer digital milestones, and impacts the way we mobilize, engage and enhance the human component. This is particularly evident in the way many are actively implementing updated workforce models such as hybrid working, more autonomous decentralized organizations and more empowered leaders at all levels. That leaves big questions for many organizations to ask themselves at board and C-suite levels:

- What do our customers expect of us now and over the next decade?

- What do our employees and other stakeholders expect of their executive leaders and board over the next decade?

- What new governance measures do we need to adopt with respect to new working models like distributed leadership, hybrid working, the blended workforce and sustainability responsibilities, as far as our Environmental Social Governance (ESG) and Social Development Goals (SDGs) are concerned?

- What specific skillsets and modern workplace know-how do we need our executive board directors and NEDs to bring to the table?

- How digitally mature are we as a board and how does that translate into reimagined strategy definition and execution?

- What experience does our board have concerning hybrid and distributed working models and the governance required for our evolving ways of working?

- How aware are we, at the board level, of the increasingly blended workforce (formalization of permanent and independent workers) and the need for a human capital framework that is fitter for purpose than a "permanent-only" model of HR management?

- How do we adapt our organizational culture to support distributed leadership and a genuine sense of empowered working across all employees, whether they are permanent or contracted independent workers?

- How does this shape our strategy at organizational senior leadership and line management levels?

- What new structural pillars do we need to establish in support of leaders at all levels?

- How do we adapt our learning and development strategy to fuel the new knowledge, skills and behaviors required of leaders at all levels?

- What new learning and development do we need at the executive board and C-suite levels to help us better navigate the future and our newly empowered workforce?

- How comfortable are we with a flatter structure and a more empowered workforce?

- Who are the new breed of NEDs and advisers who can better support our business over the next decade?

- What is our role as a board in supporting and governing a structural overhaul to make more autonomous, empowered working a reality?

It will be imperative that any adviser to a business with a flatter structure, driving leadership at all levels, rapidly adopting digital, embracing new ways of working and adapting to the changing shape of the workforce, is both experienced in this new environment and thoroughly bought into its potential.

They need to have a proven track record advising leaders in the new corporate era, rather than relying on traditional, twentieth-century legacy thinking and ways of operating. They will need to advise specifically on governance evolution and the financial underpinning of this brave new way of working, including developing a location-free mentality to unlock borderless talent integration, service offerings, customer experiences and business operations.

This raises the question of readiness for some existing NEDs, executive board members, senior leaders and the business as a whole. Are they ready to adapt? Are they ready to adopt new models, new ways of working and more? Or are they still locked into twentieth-century thinking and, thus, slowing down the transformation of the organization they are supposed to be leading or advising?

Rapid evolution is driving more empowerment through organizations. Why? Because it cannot happen without everyone contributing to the whole, as much as within their job role. It's a more collective and collaborative mindset, supported by committed executive leaders who take hold of the strategic navigation of the organization, focusing on the big picture.

Those making a lot of false starts and those who are sticking with traditional leadership approaches – micromanaging their employees, and practicing command and control, rather than unleashing and empowering people – are slow to transform. This *must* change. Therefore, "readiness" at the executive leader, NED, strategic adviser and management level is key to unlocking a new age of empowerment in organizations, as well as unleashing the inner CEOs across businesses and embracing the growth potential that leaders at all levels will deliver.

If the executive team members are not ready, are slow to act, or are only just starting their own transformational journey, this will impact the level of true empowerment that will be granted and the commitment to making distributed leadership a reality. With strong board governance and support, willing and able senior leaders and a strongly aligned operational management, the foundation pillars are in place to accelerate the shift to a new age of empowerment and autonomy at all levels.

A mindset and culture shift

As one of the top 100 law firms in the US, Baker Donelson is part of a sector known for traditional structures and practices. Yet the firm has spearheaded empowerment through a more distributed leadership model, led from the top by its CEO, Tim Lupinacci. He describes what his own role in this transformation is:

> "Part of making this whole thing work – at the board, leadership, managerial and individual contributor level – is to help everyone know that I am committed as a CEO. I will walk the talk and I have everyone's backs as they embrace something I call public empowerment. If the CEO or C-suite are not committed, it simply won't work.
>
> [...] employees at Baker Donelson know I have their backs. That takes the fear of failure, or doing things wrong away and empowers them mentally as much as in the workplace."

There are a few considerations that executive leaders should think through in seeking to create the conditions to successfully unleash the inner CEOs in their organizations and make distributed leadership and ownership a reality. To build a strong foundation for this reality, I would urge boards, NEDs and executive leaders to work through these twelve decisive questions before they do anything else:

The Decisive Dozen

1. Is the company, and am I as a senior leader, ready for this?

2. How do we ensure aligned attitudes and behaviors at the executive leadership level and across our line managers, to best enable and support unleashing the inner CEOs in the organization?

3. How do our current company values and behaviors need to evolve, to create the right culture for a new age of genuine empowerment in our organization?

4. How high is the trust level in our organization when considering the perception of our executive leadership team and line management?

5. How will we create the conditions that will allow individual contributors to leave their comfort zone and unleash their inner CEO?

6. What role will HR play in owning and supporting this process for our workforce (permanent and independent workers alike)?

7. How do we create a solid foundation of psychological safety to enable experimentation, openness, risk-taking and willing collaboration?

8. How do the executive leadership team and line managers "catch people doing it right" and sponsor further those making rapid progress?

9. What new reward and recognition elements will have the biggest impact when our people unleash their inner CEO, make progress and succeed?

10. What are the new rules of the road, processes, line management practices, learning paths and supporting infrastructure that we need to enable a truly empowered workforce?

11. What is our plan to move from words to actions and implement our vision for empowered distributed leadership?

12. What are our measures for success and how will we know we are making progress?

People at every level will need coaching and training to understand and embrace this mammoth operational and mental shift. They will need new skills and behaviors to transform the organization and themselves. They will need to be supported by a thoroughly committed executive leadership team, a flatter structure and line managers who embrace a growth mindset, as described in the earlier interview with Natasha Prasad.

It may seem like this new era requires everyone to be a superhero. In some ways, this is true. The good news is that everyone can be more engaged and empowered. It simply takes a willingness and desire to wake up, recognize and develop these core traits that we all possess as part of our human potential. It starts with an attitude that becomes part of the organizational DNA and culture. This culture enables those willing to step up to do so safely, with controlled risk and support from an equally motivated and refocused management team.

Creating the organizational conditions for success

Successfully transforming the organization has to start with decentralizing authority. A flat organization cuts through some of the clutter of hierarchical responsibility and project ownership, so it becomes localized within your teams. In addition, those teams, in turn, have greater autonomy to collaborate and make decisions that directly affect the daily operations without consulting leaders higher up, and can regularly try out new ideas and engage in innovative thinking. Here's Tim Lupinacci again, sharing a great metaphor for empowerment that he has innovated at Baker Donelson:

> "I created physical batons like you'd find in a
> running race, to represent the distribution of
> my leadership and the empowering of others

to 'run with it'. I added our logo to each baton and put my name on it. I call each person from our senior executive team up to the front of the room and hand a baton to them. It's a metaphor not just for taking responsibility, but for being accountable for leadership values, behaviors and actions, both to ourselves and to others. Each person with a baton now knows that the CEO has personally empowered them and that they are now, in turn, going to pass the baton – along with aligned and consistent expectations, commitment and support – to others who will have to be responsible for their performance. They have this responsibility alongside their manager, who in turn coaches to help them experiment, take action and achieve."

This represents the movement from a mindset shift to a collective, positive, empowered action. Once the mindset shift has taken place, you'll find that organizational culture can more easily evolve to unlock progress. If you don't have a culture that is embracing and accepting of this new process (with each person taking ownership and leading at their level), this will negatively impact the entire business and your transformation will quickly fizzle out. Organizational culture evolution is key.

Distributing authority means you need to think about the structure of your organization and whether it is ready to facilitate leadership at all levels. Have you got too many levels of hierarchy? How do you break down traditional hierarchies and flatten the structures? How do you drive a culture of empowerment and the mentality of ownership, right through the organization?

I'd recommend applying the Five-Point Star model from Chapter 2 to the organization as a whole and the executive leadership team. This will help identify what needs to happen to build an environment in which autonomous, empowered work can thrive; and where flatter management structures move leader and manager focus to performance support rather than supervision. On the importance of culture, Ehecatl Hunt-Duarte said:

> "I like to be able to help people when I can.
> Because I wasn't being put under pressure,
> I was able to make the choice to go above
> and beyond. That's to do with having a good
> workplace culture. If you don't like where you
> work, you don't feel motivated to stay there."

To further enable this evolution of culture, as we covered in Chapter 1, we must transform the whole organization and enable bold structural and human change with a strong digital thread. As Milvio DiBartolemeo puts it, empowerment at this level means that individual contributors can significantly scale up their impact:

> "[I had] the ability to influence change across
> organizational boundaries... and bring mea-
> surable improvement to the team, business

unit and to the organization, and also [I had] the opportunity to be supported and to have the confidence of senior management to continuously improve ways of working."

Great examples of companies enabling this are Zappos, Gumroad and Medium.com, as covered in an article by William Craig. His parting words should resonate for all organizations looking to empower in-role CEOs:

"... the people who perform the most important work within your organization should be doing more of the thinking about how your company will meet its future success... Innovation doesn't just happen at the CEO or upper-management levels, after all. It can happen anywhere, but it takes the right kind of leadership to foster it."[25]

To achieve this kind of leadership and the empowerment that results, it's essential to recognize the era we are working in, the pace of change and the digital technologies, tools and ways of working that can accelerate success. Haiilo (previously Smarp) – the employee engagement technology solutions company – say that almost half of mid-market firms believe that digital transformation is key to employee empowerment. This means giving everyone the right tools and tech so that they can collaborate, communicate and take ownership, and do this quickly.

The new organizational structure

While there are significant benefits to flattening the structure, we also need to acknowledge the potential downsides. For example, Zappos took apart the organizational structure and introduced its holacracy. They have since backed away from that as it didn't work going all out like that. The principle of creating flatter structures is sound, but there still has to be governance and management oversight.[26] Naturally, each organization will be different. You'll have to consider the disadvantages and have plans to mitigate these in place, along with robust rules for moving forward.

Once the new organizational structure is established, the ownership for operationalizing the new structure and approach must sit across two traditional functions. The first is organizational development and design (OD), which as a function looks at the ongoing structure of the organization and how it works, and then at how managers and teams step up, implement and action the new way forward. This has to be led by the second function, HR. If you get this right, you will unleash the in-role CEOs across your organization. You will support them with the right tools, line management support, learning and training to help them transcend their job role and contribute more broadly to the organization's operational and strategic imperatives.

Figure 7 demonstrates the speed of transformation and the level of empowerment across any organization, and the likely result in both positive and negative terms.

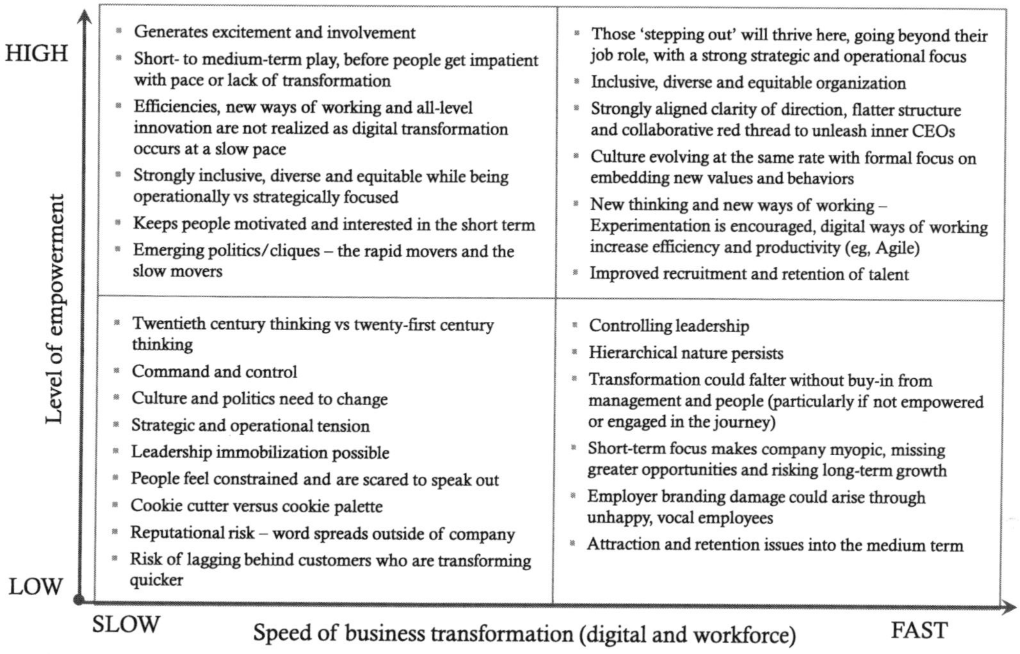
HIGH
LOW
Level of empowerment
Generates excitement and involvement
Short- to medium-term play, before people get impatient with pace or lack of transformation
Efficiencies, new ways of working and all-level innovation are not realized as digital transformation occurs at a slow pace
Strongly inclusive, diverse and equitable while being operationally vs strategically focused
Keeps people motivated and interested in the short term
Emerging politics/cliques – the rapid movers and the slow movers
Those 'stepping out' will thrive here, going beyond their job role, with a strong strategic and operational focus
Inclusive, diverse and equitable organization
Strongly aligned clarity of direction, flatter structure and collaborative red thread to unleash inner CEOs
Culture evolving at the same rate with formal focus on embedding new values and behaviors
New thinking and new ways of working – Experimentation is encouraged, digital ways of working increase efficiency and productivity (eg, Agile)
Improved recruitment and retention of talent
Twentieth century thinking vs twenty-first century thinking
Command and control
Culture and politics need to change
Strategic and operational tension
Leadership immobilization possible
People feel constrained and are scared to speak out
Cookie cutter versus cookie palette
Reputational risk – word spreads outside of company
Risk of lagging behind customers who are transforming quicker
Controlling leadership
Hierarchical nature persists
Transformation could falter without buy-in from management and people (particularly if not empowered or engaged in the journey)
Short-term focus makes company myopic, missing greater opportunities and risking long-term growth
Employer branding damage could arise through unhappy, vocal employees
Attraction and retention issues into the medium term
SLOW
Speed of business transformation (digital and workforce)
FAST

Figure 7: *Speed of transformation and relative level of empowered people*

This four-box model should be used as part of the early discussions at the executive board and C-suite levels. It helps to focus the discussion on readiness, through to what is happening at an organization level, considering both the speed of transformation with current (or desired) levels of empowerment.

As an example, using this model, if your speed of transformation is slow and your level of empowerment low, then you may have a twentieth-century-thinking business, not a twenty-first-century one. This creates strategic and operational tension and people will typically feel constrained. By comparison, when you're highly empowered and moving at a fast pace, this creates an inclusive and diverse environment in leadership terms. This pace of change naturally requires collaborative leaders at all levels, with a culture appropriate for the modern era.

As another example, if you are slow but driving high levels of empowerment, there is a balance of short-term excitement mixed with medium- to long-term frustration, as transformation does not keep pace with in-role CEOs who wish to push boundaries and speed up change. This could lead to increased workplace politics, old-style management reappearing and, worse, talent being disillusioned and leaving the company. A negative cycle is hard to break when your people, who are being empowered, are thinking in twenty-first-century terms, while the organization is stuck in the twentieth century and making slow progress.

Getting the mix right and then creating an environment in which distributed leadership can thrive – where empowered autonomy and a more supportive management structure unleash the power and potential of the many – comes down to the human component. This means a culture shift in how everybody engages, communicates and collaborates, often transcending job descriptors, roles or functional lines, that then becomes the norm.

Those who intend to be the successful companies of the future must train their people to unleash their inner CEO so that they are empowered and prepared to take autonomous action. Typically, they will need them not only to upskill but also to think differently. It's up to executive leaders, HR and line management to create the conditions of psychological safety, inclusion, trust and empowerment so that their people can embrace this mindset themselves.

Getting to this point means you have OD owning the new structure, and new ways of working in the business. You've also got human talent leaders, HR and others communicating what's going to happen and upskilling everybody involved, so they're owning and correctly enabling this culture of empowerment. This is important because, if support, training and coaching are approached in the same way as they would be for individuals' core job roles, it's not going to work. Therefore, organizational development and training must also evolve.

Implications for line managers

As well as processes and skills for the people who are unleashing their inner CEO, you'll need to empower the existing line managers by equipping them with new skills to support these newly unleashed leaders. They need to learn how to support, how to develop and how to provide the unleashed leaders with management and leadership insight. The line managers for potential in-role CEOs will become the conduit between the action and the impact of that action on others, the business and the growth of the individual.

There are two key component actions for the organization's line management: first, to make sure everyone still performs in their core role; and second, to be the enablers behind those unleashing their inner CEO. This often requires competency frameworks or talent management processes, which will need to be refreshed to identify what these capabilities are in terms of knowledge, skills and behaviors.

For those who are willing to step in, step out or step up, an initial collaboration discussion using the Five-Point Star assessment framework needs to take place to ascertain suitability and competence and to identify strengths and skill gaps. This will help each person in the organization be a part of the discussion and agree with their line manager whether stepping in, out or up is the most suitable approach for them.

This, in turn, becomes a powerful line management tool, combining a core job developmental focus with increased attention on the new, more strategic knowledge, skills and behaviors we want our in-role

CEOs to embrace and develop. These unique support structures can be put in place for individuals to create a development plan. The first six months will require feedback loops and coaching to facilitate close support for those unleashing their inner CEO. At the organizational level, a structured reporting process is required that accurately measures the improvement, ongoing strengths and gaps in the unleashed population as they evolve in their roles.

The structure becomes a fluid personal development plan that is owned at the organizational level by HR, then enacted through the line manager, while ultimately being owned by in-role CEOs themselves, so they are working on building the skills they need to demonstrate leadership and management capabilities. This should be central to how they will be measured, recognized and rewarded in their new role, and what that means for their potential career path. That career path could be within the job role or a part of a fast-tracked leadership pipeline journey, depending on the person, their motivations and their stretch.

Reward and recognition structures

Flattening the overall structure comes with many benefits because you're building ownership of the business within each role throughout the organization. But – and here comes one of the major "cons" – if I am someone who has unleashed my inner CEO and I look at the organization and see a flattened hierarchy, I won't see many levels above me, and I can't see a defined career path. Therefore, while a new job title may not be forthcoming, a clear infrastructure for recognition and reward must be. This is central to employee satisfaction, building resilience and embedding a feeling of inclusion and belonging. In-role CEO Milvio DiBartolemeo cites resilience and reward as critical for successful empowerment:

"The two most important factors for me are resilience and the ability to continue from any setback or blockers, particularly when proposing a new way of thinking based on industry best practices and also from a career perspective. This was a driver for me to continue my professional development and a point of difference from anyone in the market. Also, appreciation and gratitude from my line manager for the work and effort to go beyond. This resulted in greater flexibility and other non-financial rewards."

Therefore, any organization committed to unleashing their inner CEOs and sponsoring leadership at all levels must think about how to recognize and reward new behaviors, emerging skills and those making an impact beyond their job role as they contribute to broader business health. Having a properly thought-through recognition approach will help to minimize the "con" above and place a value on the desired organizational change. This will ensure those stepping up remain satisfied in their role as they develop and grow as described by Ehecatl Hunt-Duarte:

"Recognition of achievement is important and it shouldn't go unnoticed. When time has been freed up because of efficiencies created, this should be recognized with a reward... Everyone recognizes achievement where I work. I don't think I work to receive recognition and kudos, but it is motivating when it happens. We have a 'celebrating success' culture."

For many, this will represent an ideal situation, as they no longer feel the pressure or need to be promoted, while still having the ability to contribute in the longer term at their level, in their role, to the broader strategic aims of the business. This can solve generational issues and "long-termer fatigue", and may ultimately be a more inclusive and valued policy.

Below are some of the tactics to consider as the organization formalizes its recognition and reward approach. As you will see, rewards come in many forms. Rasie Bamigbade cites some examples that she found personally motivating during her empowerment journey:

"... feeding my ambition, growing in my role and into other roles, leading teams through new projects/challenges, support from other leaders, reaching the planned results."

The following table is a starting point to spark additional ideas suited to the organization and individuals concerned.

How to effectively recognize people/effort	Senior leadership team meeting presentation	Certification system (bronze, silver and gold in-role CEOs) based on specific measurable/provable criteria that all those unleashing their inner CEO can aspire to	Gamify the unleashing of the inner CEOs with badges/merits linked to non-monetary awards (eg, lifestyle awards)	Appointing an executive leader mentor to accompany the journey for specific projects or points in time	Inclusion in relevant strategic meetings, special projects and external events	Announcements in company events, newsletters and with customers
Non-monetary reward	Time off for wellness and personal pampering	Party or awards event for the individual and their team/collaborative group	Paid dinner for the individual with friends/partner/family	Paid holiday for the individual and their family/partner	L&D to grow strategic/leadership skills (outside of normal learning path)	Trips and visits to other parts of the company (globally) to share best practices and experiences
Monetary rewards	Bonus based on qualitative and quantitative impact on the business and other stakeholders (rewarding both behaviours and results)	Annual increases in salary, on top of normal increase, possible up to an incremental percentage defined by the business (such as an additional 5% based on in-role CEO performance)	Bonus payment on attaining bronze, silver, gold certification as in-role CEO	Line manager discretionary budget to provide relatively small monetary bonuses during regular reviews throughout the year	CEO Special Award – a competition in parallel with other activities to identify and reward the best new initiative that has the biggest impact on the business, on people and on the customer: a large one-off cash prize and public recognition	New contract/extended contract/long-term contract for those independent freelance workers contributing with consistency and excellence to the business

Figure 8: Recognition and reward suggestions to add to your own

Having all this in place, upfront, empowers people to take ownership and be recognized for new behaviors, for measurable progress and for the new results they pull through.

What next?

In the next chapter, I'll set out a practical framework of operational steps to follow, to support individual contributors and line managers to embrace in-role leadership.

But first, our next interview highlights the experience of Steen Puggaard, executive board member, equity investor and CEO. Steen shares his journey as an entrepreneur and owner, of unleashing, as he calls them, "mini-CEOs". He describes the organizational conditions and actions he implemented to achieve this, and how his mini-CEOs have helped him to grow success.

Interview with Steen Puggaard

Steen Puggaard has supported and started many successful businesses, including the 4Fingers Crispy Chicken food chain. He was an early investor and former CEO of the business, which he grew from one outlet in Singapore to several across the region, with a revenue of more than $40m annually, bucking the trend of how fast food could be provided and managed.

From the outset, Steen was committed to unleashing leadership at the store level and from day one appointed what he calls "mini-CEOs".

JEREMY: At 4Fingers, you clearly identified people who could contribute to the broader business success, beyond their job role. How did you go about creating the environment for this mindset to flourish?

STEEN: The starting point was to instill in people the sense that we're all in charge of our own destiny. I gave people a very clear vision and a sense of where we were going, how we were planning to do it and what I expected from them, including how I'd ensure they were supported. This was a big motivating factor, and we reached a place where I could say to them, "Conquer that hill," and I knew I could rely on them to do it.

But it is a journey, and some people won't make it. That's why it is so much about the right stuff that is already within people, underpinned by upskilling and a willingness to grab opportunities, even when the going gets tough. I even used the term "mini-CEO", rather than saying "restaurant general manager". It sowed different aspirations in people to think it, own it and do it.

Some people didn't get it and saw a "title", and with that they assumed entitlement. They didn't see the need for the mini-CEO state of mind, backed up by an evolving skillset and the need to deliver results above and beyond their job role. But in most cases, at 4Fingers, it worked well. I really believed in bothering my mini-CEOs as little as possible, once they knew the direction and what was expected. That way, it was easy to spot who stepped up.

JEREMY: Fast-food service outlets have to be consistent and repetitive in what they do and how they do things. But you created a framework for this empowerment to happen within the scope of your business. This tells us that it's possible even in regulated, compliance-led, niche, cookie-cutter industries. What do you think?

STEEN: I absolutely agree. Once you know what your business is about at its simplest level, you can build around it and create broader opportunities for people to contribute. The core business was relatively simple, and I always said we needed to do two things excellently.

First, on a macro level, you figure out what it takes to run one store successfully. How do we build it? How do we prepare? How do we staff it? What does the customer journey look like? And then you thoroughly document that. The rest is just scaling up as you add new outlets and concepts; you re-use the cookie cutter.

Second, you find out what it takes to serve one customer really well, and then you scale it up and strive to continually improve on that customer journey.

JEREMY: As a leader, what must be in place at the team leadership level to enable an environment where people embrace what you're saying and unleash their inner CEO?

STEEN: First of all, it's about the person in charge – the company's CEO needs to profoundly buy into the philosophy. Otherwise, it will never work. Back in the '80s, there was the fantastic turnaround story of Scandinavian Airlines. The company had been heading toward potential bankruptcy for a number of years, due to oil crises, cross-airline competition and so on. The board, in a last-ditch attempt at a turnaround, decided to bring in an outsider to the traditional airline industry for a different perspective. They approached Jan Carlzon, who ran a charter travel agency, and asked him if he would run the company.

He took the job and the first thing he did was to round up the head office staff in one of the aircraft hangars. He brought in a portable aircraft stepladder, climbed it and introduced himself as their new CEO. He confessed that he didn't know anything about running an airline, but he knew that they all did and that he was looking forward to receiving everyone's suggestions for how to improve the business.[27]

JEREMY: What needs to happen at line management level to commit to CEO role modeling, taking ownership and empowering others?

STEEN: My ability to build any company depends on my ability to go out and attract the right people and to spend time identifying and appealing to those who I believe will be giants for the company's situation now, and who can steer success as it grows in the future. When you can engage people in the journey, excite and help motivate them, it's half the battle.

JEREMY: That demonstrates the importance of having this strong, open-minded leadership and empowering culture, doesn't it?

STEEN: Someone once said that if you don't intentionally shape your company culture, the culture will tend to shape itself. When I build a culture dedicated to excellence and people working together, it runs itself.

JEREMY: As a westerner living and working in Singapore for more than twenty years, did you discern the culture differences with regard to driving ownership through the organization?

STEEN: I did screw up a couple of times by being too "western" in my approach early on in my time in Asia. There are certain tactics I find useful for Asia, such as the need to be more succinct and not ramble on as some leaders in western organizations do.

In food and beverage businesses across Asia, the typical employee turnover rate is between 70% and 100%. Nearly all your staff would leave within twelve months. But we reduced it to less than 25% turnover across our key worker population. To support the culture, I use the cost of attrition to create a budget for salary increases and loyalty bonuses, to reward the people who consistently contribute. It creates a positive buzz and reduces the cost of attrition.

JEREMY: And did your customers buy into the 4Fingers philosophy?

STEEN: It's about creating a brand. The brand, for me, is the best way to create value because people say, "I'll pay more for that because it is brand ABC." Brand won when we hit 100,000 followers on Facebook, and there were 5,000 people who not only liked but also posted to engage with the brand. The secret sauce was not on our chicken; it was in our staff.

JEREMY: Based on these amazing experiences as CEO, investor and entrepreneur, what advice would you give leaders about unleashing their inner CEOs and driving new levels of success?

STEEN: The first thing is to be crystal clear about your destination because without a destination you will never arrive. The second thing is to understand the culture of the business and how empowered, or otherwise, your people feel, in readiness to buy into the vision of unleashing their inner CEO. The third element would be to quickly get the buy-in from your management team, who will be responsible for making it happen.

Be clear about the vision and what the business is trying to achieve and how you shape targets, style and co-working, to ensure consistency and alignment as you implement. As a leader, getting buy-in from your team is essential. A leader without followers is just a guy walking.

I have seen this approach work. I'd wager there will be increases in shareholder value, employer brand value, employee and customer satisfaction for companies that unleash their inner CEOs.

FOUR

Making It Happen

I n this chapter, which is about unleashing leadership at all levels, we'll cover:

- The traits of an in-role CEO

- The 4Es Distributed Leadership model and Assessment for in-role CEOs

- My 90-Day Road Map to supercharge implementation of distributed leadership, broken down into week-by-week actions and suggestions

- A supporting personal development framework to build the in-role CEO knowledge, skills and behaviors required

In the previous chapter, we covered the organizational component of unleashing the inner CEO. Now, we'll proceed to what needs to be in place at a personal level – in other words, at the human talent level, where HR professionals and managers are empowering individual contributors and providing the foundation for greater personal autonomy, authority and action for leaders at all levels.

The traits of an in-role CEO

There are certain traits that an in-role CEO must display. I look for these traits when developing leadership at all levels in the organizations I work with, to guide them through this shift. These people are already looking ahead, as well as being "in the now". It's a delicate balance between protecting the short term and what they need to achieve in their role, while being future-minded and considering what they want and need to do next. It's like being a more operational chief executive officer.

An in-role CEO can liaise at all levels comfortably, internally and externally. This may take practice for those who have not been used to displaying or encouraged to show this kind of initiative. The successful employee of the future must also take calculated risks, with the support of management, because this is going to be increasingly important. They have to be able to communicate and sell their ideas in terms of developing the business case. An important question for in-role CEOs to ask themselves is, "How do I engage others in the journey so I can execute successfully and be supported in striving for better solutions and innovation?"

Potential in-role CEOs mustn't be set up for failure. They must be empowered to implement their ideas and have a mobilized team around them: they need a support infrastructure that will help them to accelerate success and growth. This applies to both permanent and independent workers, who together comprise the blended workforce of the digital era, working together and taking ownership for the ultimate success of the company – as well as within their job role. Senior leaders can make a difference by seeing everyone as having the potential to unleash their inner CEO, rather than confining individual contributors to rigid job descriptions, and must help them to create early wins.

That is why the evolving workplace offers a much more exciting opportunity for independent thinkers, whether within a corporate structure or self-employment. In the new diverse workforce, both permanent and independent workers who have not traditionally been the beneficiaries of this kind of sponsorship will be able to enjoy more freedom in their decision-making and creativity. The time is ripe for recruiting and harnessing the abundant talent already available within and outside corporate confines. We no longer have to be constrained by a traditional permanent workforce and can explore more creative operating models and ways of working.

To achieve this, first, it's important for those stepping in, stepping out or stepping up to be willing and able to take ownership of their development. Second, they will need to be ready and able to develop a network of peer and management-level contacts as a support infrastructure while growing in their role. Also, guidelines need to be in place for building skills and assessing and tracking progress, as candidates embrace the new vision and develop their leadership and management capabilities. What's required is a development plan to take your people forward for at least the first ninety days. Everyone has the potential to unleash their inner CEO, and they need to be part of the discussion early on. This will help to understand their preferences, any support needed and how the individual sees themselves stepping in, stepping out or stepping up.

The models and frameworks that follow together provide a comprehensive toolkit to support the development and growth of in-role CEOs.

The 4Es Distributed Leadership model

The 4Es Distributed Leadership model brings together the four key themes of the assessment: Envision, Engage, Execute and Excel. These four components are proven to support and enable distributed leadership success.

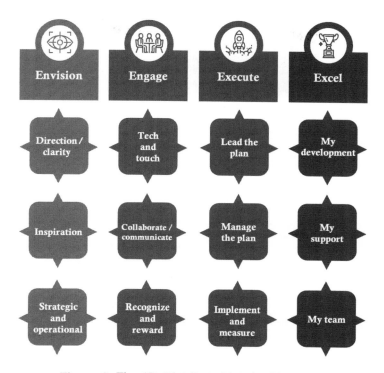

Figure 9: *The 4Es Distributed Leadership model*

Envision

Those ready to unleash their inner CEO first need to "Envision". This comprises three key areas.

Direction and clarity

Having direction means being able to clearly articulate an intention regardless of the audience – whether up the line, down the line or across lines. Questions to consider are:

- What is the goal?

- What does success look like?

- Is everyone clear on what needs to be done?

Inspiration

Potential in-role CEOs need to act like leaders and be able to inspire others in their own distinctive way. Individuals may have (or think they have) a brilliant idea, but if the ability to both elicit support from others up the line and engage a collaborative group to help with execution is missing, then the projects of unleashed CEOs may fail before they've begun. Success requires an ability to motivate and display a good balance of emotional intelligence (EQ) as well as traditional IQ.

I've found that what makes truly great (versus average) leaders is the emotional and personal side of the relationship. It's the ability to be more self-aware about how one is behaving, acting and affecting others in the organization. Good questions for prospective in-role CEOs to ask themselves are:

- How do you manage yourself?

- Are you able to empathize with and motivate others?

- How do you bring everybody together?

This is the type of leadership that makes a real difference. If you think of the best leaders you have worked with in your career, what are the traits that make them a great leader? Typically, it's not only that they hit their targets, but more about the emotions that your interactions with them provoke. It's great to work with these leaders. There's a feeling that they get you and have got your back – it feels good.

Strategic and operational outlook

The third area is about having an eye on the sky and feet on the ground: a combination of strategic and operational understanding. The strategic component is a new idea or project that aligns with the direction of the overall business, contributing beyond job role, team and even function. It involves considering how a new idea will affect the business. The operational component follows and focuses on what execution by in-role CEOs will look like, including the mobilization of appropriate resources and the support needed to implement the idea or project successfully.

I repeat: in-role CEOs have to have *both strategic and operational outlooks*, not just one or the other. They have to think differently; this is strategic, critical and creative thinking all rolled into one. There's a need to review progress, navigate the route, problem-solve and be flexible and adaptable as development progresses.

Engage

The second component is the ability to "Engage" others, which is also made up of three key components.

Tech and touch

The first aspect of engaging others on this journey of unleashing the inner CEO is knowing how to bring people along with you. In-role CEOs must know which digital tools are appropriate and available, and be confident in using them. They must use them to enhance the human touch, helping to connect people in new ways, for communication, clarity and collaboration. This will undoubtedly require supportive training, coaching and skill development.

Collaborate and communicate

We are entering an era of more collective leadership, and this is enabling greater collaboration and more open communication. Many individual contributors are already being asked to be part of cross-functional projects, as well as being encouraged within their teams – and supported by peer coaching – to collaborate and collectively own tasks, objectives and goals. The rise of self-driven or self-owned teams has been a mainstay of the technology sector for many years, leading to more agile working methods – scrums, sprints and more. It's only recently that other industries, teams, co-workers and so on have woken up to the power of collaboration.

The combination of the digital and the human elevates collaboration and communication to a higher level, which means that an idea can be executed much faster. The in-role CEO needs to know how to communicate effectively and create strong, collaborative teams.

Recognize and reward

The role of recognition and reward features just as heavily as it always has in leadership. As we've already seen, people are more engaged when they are recognized for their efforts. This is an aspect of human touch that hasn't changed. Overall, a lot will be expected of newly empowered individuals in the future workforce, so how will the company reward this effort and contribution? What does it mean, and how will managers and leaders make sure it happens? How are in-role CEOs going to be rewarded for embracing this new leadership challenge? This is an important conversation for every corporate leader, HR professional, line manager and individual contributor to have. (See Chapter 3 for ideas about how organizations can recognize and reward in-role CEOs.)

In-role CEOs also have a responsibility toward the people collaborating with them when they are doing an amazing job, and it is important to consider their role in recognizing the increased contribution from the wider workforce.

Execute

The third element requires an in-role CEO to be implementation-minded and "Execute" effectively and efficiently, usually with others. Again, there are three components central to success:

Lead the plan

Successful execution requires continued leadership to maintain focus on the plan and understand how the project will work, with agreed milestones and measurable actions. This makes the vision and plan clear to all stakeholders, including the customer or internal client, who all must be engaged and aligned with the way forward. Then the focus can shift to executing and managing the plan.

Manage the plan

According to Marc Kelly, VP at Gartner, "sixty-one percent of corporate strategists say poor strategy execution is the primary reason that new growth initiatives fail."[28] Why? Poor execution, poor communication and poor momentum building. It's all about managing the implementation and actions.

Being able to manage the tasks and the key people in the team is central to steering the success of your overall project plan. Regular reviews of tasks, progress and next steps will be required, in parallel with formalized team reviews and one-to-one sessions with the stakeholders involved.

In-role CEOs must also be technically competent to manage a project timeline and use the appropriate technology and tools, which are constantly evolving. This will heighten the need for collaboration and the consistency and frequency of communication, which must also be a central part of the plan. Not only that, being project-minded will support the leadership and management of the team as much as the tasks. Everything will be visible to all involved, which shares the responsibilities and accountabilities beyond the person leading the project. This is very much in the spirit of distributed leadership and allows everyone to contribute and own their piece of the project. It is the golden thread that will drive success.

Implement and measure actions

Getting the leadership plan and the management principles behind the plan in place represent big first steps forward for implementation success. This will accelerate actions and help the project or task leader to build momentum. Establishing measurement milestones will also be important to keep everyone involved motivated and on track, to enable them to own their part of it and continue moving forward.

In parallel, it's essential to have what I call a "solution mindset". This is about knowing and accepting that there will be bumps and diversions along the way while remaining focused on what is possible, rather than what can't be done. There may even be new information or actions that lead to new thinking. The project leader and team should be open to adapting their plan as they move forward if there are clear benefits to doing so. Of course, any adaptations will come with new actions and measures that should be tracked. For in-role CEOs, this means thinking about how to drive action, celebrate early wins, track measures and overcome problems quickly, escalating the problem when needed.

Excel

The final component, "Excel", is about the development of those individuals on the journey to unleash their inner CEO and demonstrate leadership. There are three areas they will need to consider:

1. My development

2. My support

3. My team

My development

All in-role CEOs, regardless of whether they are stepping in, stepping out or stepping up, should own their development, with strong support from organizational functions like HR and learning and development, alongside line manager support and leadership mentorship where relevant or appropriate.

The personal development journey is underpinned by emotional and social intelligence, as in-role CEOs continue to learn how to manage both tasks and interpersonal interactions effectively. This will ultimately define their level of success. As such, any in-role CEO should ask themselves the following questions and consider going through them with their line manager as part of the "My support" component of the fourth E (Excel).

- Am I willing and able to embark on an accelerated personal learning and development journey?

- What do I need to know; what do I need to do (differently); and what behaviors will benefit my evolution into an in-role CEO?

- Am I open, trusted by and supportive of others?

- Am I aware of how I am operating and coming across to others?

- Am I going to do what I say, to execute, support others and lead the project, task or idea to implementation success?

- What do I need to do, and to model, to excel as a leader, regardless of my job description and day-to-day role?

This expansive, self-aware mindset is essential for in-role CEOs to excel while being part of the new, empowered organization of the future.

This is explored further in Chapter 6 through my new model, the Six Centers of Me. This is made up of six topics on which to reflect, so that we can measure the behavioral and personal development success of unleashing our inner CEOs, in parallel with the quantitative project, task and individual measures already in place.

My support

This component reflects both the support that any in-role CEO receives (for example, from their line manager, leadership mentor, peer coaches and project partners) and the support they provide to those they are working and collaborating with.

The support infrastructure will be a defining part of the success, and there is a risk of failure if it is not in place. Some useful questions for in-role CEOs to discuss with line support managers include:

- Have I asked those I will be working with what their preferences are in terms of my support, communication and ways of interacting?

- Am I prepared to flex my own style to better work with and support others?

- What do I need from task or project collaborators to support me, my actions and my personal development?

- What do I need in terms of support and development "on the job" from my line manager and other senior stakeholders?

- How do I establish a formalized feedback process, whereby everyone feels psychologically safe to initiate or take part in open and honest discussions?

- How do I know I am developing personally?

- How do I know I am effectively and successfully contributing to team or project group development?

My team

This component represents a mindset shift from "me" to "we" so that our in-role CEOs are focused on creating a climate whereby collaboration and communication effectiveness are central to team success as much as individual achievement. For any in-role CEO, this component is critical for progressing work with others, engaging them in the journey and motivating them to perform, as they contribute to the ultimate success of the project or task at hand.

To facilitate this, in-role CEOs will benefit from developing a coaching mindset to support individuals as they focus on getting the job done. They should also ask themselves some critical questions to shape their mindset and interpersonal skillsets:

- How do we work together as a high-performing team?

- How can we focus on our goal to successfully implement the plan?

- How do I support others in achieving results?

- How do I flex my style to build stronger, more personalized relationships?

- How do I sharpen up my emotional and social intelligence?

- How can I recognize that the members of my project team are other in-role CEOs, with the capability to lead their part of the project, for the benefit of the whole?

Ultimately, in-role CEOs must model the desired behaviors and skills required and be prepared to support those who are on the journey with them. This will engage others more effectively and build a winning team mentality with an action orientation.

The 4Es assessment

To underpin the importance of the 4Es, I offer an online assessment to all my clients. You can also contact me directly to access the online assessment and other resources. The outputs from this assessment can be supported by a series of vital questions to ask at each step (below), which will help facilitate coaching discussions and uncover the most appropriate support and developmental interventions to put in place. This is how to build a road map for success.

Employees or independent workers will be able to apply the 4Es Distributed Leadership model by themselves as an online assessment, but I recommend it is also completed as 180-degree feedback. Alternatively, 360-degree feedback can be gathered where appropriate to curate further inputs for the ongoing development of in-role CEOs. As a rough guide for how and when to use the assessments, I would suggest:

- **Those stepping in:** Self-assessment or 180-degree assessment.

- **Those stepping out:** 180- or 360-degree assessment among their team and function.

- **Those stepping up:** 360-degree assessment incorporating management and leadership sponsor voices, as well as a mix of those the individual is collaborating and working with. This feedback is collected from within their team and function, or outside of it.

The assessment consists of thirty-six statements around the 4Es, aiming to establish where someone is comfortable, where they are not and what needs to be in place so that they can start making positive changes. Once completed, it can be returned to from time to time as a quantifiable measure of personal growth, impact on others and impact on the business. The statements are closely related to the supporting key questions below, to ensure that the assessment itself is linked to the follow-up discussions, ongoing coaching and personal development. For in-role CEOs, this is the way to own that development.

Instead of completing the online assessment, Figures 10–13 present the key development questions designed to accompany the assessment as a coaching guide, bring out the reasons for certain assessment outcomes and help identify strengths and development gaps. They are framed first for the individual to consider as self-reflection, and then to discuss with their line manager, facilitating joint discussion, coaching moments and inspiration.

This process of consideration, discussion and planning makes the whole process a highly practical one and will help fast-track immediate next steps, developmental actions and any other initial support required. Overall, this will lead to a more considered and personalized development plan, as part of the first 90-Day Road Map to becoming an in-role CEO.

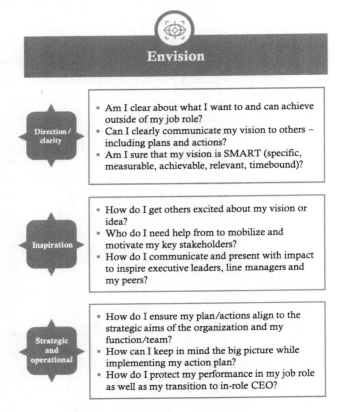

Figure 10: *Questions for Envision*

Engage

Tech and touch

- What technology and new ways of working are available within my business to support internal communications and collaboration?
- What technologies and tools are easiest to use and implement for maximum positive impact?
- How do I ensure quality one-to-one time (face-to-face or virtual) with individuals supporting/working with me?

Collaborate / communicate

- What is the formula for winning collaboration internally and externally?
- How do I enable a collaborative, high-performing work group?
- What formal and informal communication needs to be in place to maximize buy-in, action and measurable impact?

Recognize and reward

- How do I catch others doing it right?
- What do I expect from my line management to highlight my contribution, and help me recognize others'?
- Am I clear as to how the company will measure, recognize and reward in-role CEOs for successfully stepping in, stepping out or stepping up?

Figure 11: *Questions for Engage*

Execute

Lead the plan

- Have I translated my strategy into a simple, easy to communicate and execute plan (for myself and others)?
- Is every stakeholder involved clear about the plan and their role in it?
- Have I anticipated where problems/challenges could arise, and have I got a contingency plan?

Manage the plan

- What managerial skills do I need to best help me manage key tasks and stakeholders?
- How do I manage things when it's going well and how do I manage challenges and tough conversations?
- What do I expect from my manager in terms of on-the-job support and coaching?

Implement and measure

- How knowledgeable am I about problem-solving technique and execution?
- When the going gets tough or we come across roadblocks, how do I encourage others to find solutions not problems?
- How do I ensure we measure progress from day one, with clear milestones in place along the way?

Figure 12: *Questions for Execute*

Excel

My development

- Am I clear about my own strengths, gaps and action steps? (eg, 4Es assessment)
- Have I completed my first 90-day plan?
- Do I have a robust personal development plan, supported by my line manager?

My support

- How do I interact with individuals who are part of the implementation team?
- What relationship/rules of the road do I need in place with my line manager?
- Who would I value ongoing feedback from to help me develop my skill sets as formal or informal mentors and sounding boards?

My team

- How do I build and develop high-performing project/task teams?
- How do I engage other stakeholders who may not be part of the organization (partners, customers, independent workers)?
- How do I map and manage my key stakeholders from start to finish?

Figure 13: *Questions for Excel*

This thirty-six-question coaching guide will help support the personal development journey that is required to unleash the inner CEO. It is an important accompaniment to the formal online assessment and will support interactive coaching conversations between individuals, line managers and other stakeholders on that journey. This ensures that all candidates are supported, in the right way, to develop the knowledge, skills and behaviors essential for success as an in-role CEO and beyond.

The 90-Day Road Map

Designed to be modified to suit various organizational and personal needs, this road map for distributed leadership success incorporates the main activities and expected outputs for in-role CEOs as they embrace the concept and then the reality of distributed leadership.

Each person using the 90-Day Road Map should be encouraged to come up with a maximum of three new ideas or projects. It may be difficult to achieve significant progress if individuals and their line managers become overwhelmed with too many new projects in addition to their usual roles, so more than three is not advised. It's essential to unleash inner CEOs in a systematic and controlled way, rather than rush in without adequate preparation. As the road map shows, it is a step-by-step process.

Week	Main activities	Output
1	Establish parameters within which to operate. Obtain role clarity. 90- day goal and roadmap, including project focus, additional activities beyond job role and learning plan (mosaic menu). Establish senior leader as sponsor/informal mentor outside line management support. 4Es self-assessment and resulting development plan.	A mutually understood and agreed plan that can be shared across the business.
2	Initial learning activities. 4Es understanding and skills building (training and on the job coaching). Develop ideas for special projects/new ideas.	Skills gaps/strengths understanding and business case for up to two/three new ideas and projects for in-role CEO to lead.
3	Initial learning activities. 4Es understanding and skills building (training and on the job coaching). Activate new project/focus area for in-role CEO to lead.	Agree initial in-role CEO new focus areas/project. Kick off and key measures/milestones agreement.
4	Project team kick off and robust project actions. Agree mobile digital tool to drive communication/collaboration efficiencies (and reduce email), eg, Typing Mind (AI wraparound), Trello, Notion, Slack, WhatsApp. These will also help to track project progress and exchanges. Possible project management training, if available (or personally secured learning around PM principles and use of tech like Trello).	Mobilize, engage and communicate with stakeholder groups and update on objectives, measures, roles and responsibilities. Establish communications parameters/rules.

Figure 14a: *The 90-Day Roadmap, Weeks 1–4*

Weeks 1–4

The initial stage of Weeks 1–4 is about learning activities and ensuring skills building on the job. This is where a sound grasp of the 4Es model, with an assessment and development focus, is essential. It's then about moving toward the activation of one of the new projects, or the development of one of the new ideas generated, with the output agreed.

Week 1 of the 90-Day Road Map covers the operational parameters, role clarity and the 90-day goal, including the project focus. It also includes additional activities beyond the job role and learning plan. The output of the first week must be mutually understood and the plan agreed upon before sharing it across the business. Based on what's agreed, a training course may already be organized, with candidates pre-booked, so they know exactly what's coming up. It's about job coaching and developing ideas for special projects, independently and with the line manager. This is exciting because it's where unleashing the inner CEO comes alive for individuals, who will own their 90-Day Road Map and the development path that goes with it.

Week 4 is the project kick-off stage. It's essential at this point to make sure that key measures and milestones are agreed. Let's say a new project has been identified. Robust project actions are required, and you should agree on which mobile digital tools will be used to drive efficient communication and collaboration. The goal is to reduce time wasted going back and forth in the old, less productive way of working.

Tools such as Zoom, MS Teams, Google Workspace, Slack and Workplace by Facebook are all worth exploring to better connect, drive collaboration and encourage open and secure communication. These can support in-role work, project work, small collaborative groups, events management and much more. Where more formalized projects and tasks need to be managed, with multiple strands running in parallel, I recommend tools such as Trello and Notion. There are also more specialized platforms such as Asana®, Microsoft Project™ and Smartsheet® to consider.

The outputs for Weeks 1–4 are:

- Agree on the outcomes for the 90-Day Road Map

- Mobilize, engage and communicate with stakeholder groups

- Update on objectives, measures, roles and responsibilities

- Establish communications parameters and rules for the ongoing project

Weeks 5-8

Week 5 is the perfect time to review learning, actions, roadblocks, successes and what's needed for continued progress. It is an early opportunity to sit down with the line manager, project team and peer coaches to assess progress so far and identify what feedback has been received, what is working, what needs tweaking and what further support is required.

Week	Main activities	Output
5	Month 1 review – learnings, actions, roadblocks, successes and needs to go forward. Analysis of any impact on job-role focus and discussion – 4Es assessment review and personal development plan modification. Ongoing project action and communication.	Management/HR awareness of progress, successes, gaps and support requirements. Ongoing ownership of new projects and developments.
6	Possible secondment/co-working with mentor or key managers/ leaders in the business as best practice sharing and ongoing personal development for in-role CEO. Ongoing project action and communication.	An introduction to the wider business and how some key leaders and managers operate to secure best practices and add to personal in-role CEO toolkit.
7	Month 2 learning activity (formal training or on-the-job coaching sessions) – personal development mosaic actions driven by in-role CEO in parallel with company activity. Ongoing project action and communication.	Implement modified learning plan following previous week and refocus personal development on must-have leader/manager skillsets to support ongoing project management.
8	End of Month 2 stakeholder/project team reviews (progress so far on actions/initiatives, etc). Formalized feedback loop from stakeholders – temperature check re: knowledge, skills and behaviors.	Feedback useful to modify personal development plan and ongoing learning/project/stakeholder focus.

Figure 14b: *The 90-Day Roadmap, Weeks 5–8*

It's essential to include an analysis of any impact on the individual's job role because you've got to ensure that the day-to-day performance is there, not just on the new projects. At this point, it may be necessary to have a more robust discussion about the outputs of the 4Es assessment and to modify the personal development plan if appropriate. It's now possible to see the reality of what's needed as opposed to just the planning theory.

Week 6 brings us to the halfway mark and is about co-working and adopting best practices. Here we also consider what makes a great leader and a great manager, and what happens in other departments, so that candidates for in-role CEOs begin to get a broader view of what's going on throughout the company, not just in their team.

Week 7 is a good point for additional formal training and on-the-job coaching sessions to keep the momentum going. At this point, we're aiming for the personal development actions from the Personal Development Mosaic menus (in the following section) to be driven by the individual, in parallel with company activity and ongoing projects.

Week 8 is about stakeholder and project team reviews. This is the first opportunity for formal reviews. There must be a formalized feedback loop for stakeholders and temperature checks around knowledge, skills and behaviors so that you can gauge what's working and what's not. This requires the potential in-role CEO to be thinking about what needs modifying as part of their personal development plan, including the organization of ongoing personalized learning and day-to-day coaching.

The outputs for Weeks 5–8 are:

- Management and HR awareness of progress, successes, gaps and support requirements

- Ownership of actions, embedding and sharing new practices

- Implementation of the modified learning plan

- Stakeholder and project team feedback

Weeks 9–12

Week	Main activities	Output
9	Ongoing project action and communications/new learning plan initiated with on-the-job support.	Full focus on job role and special project/initiative.
10	Ongoing project action and communications/new learning plan initiated with on-the-job support.	Full focus on job role and special project/initiative.
11	Project progress measurement and consolidation with team and manager in advance of Week 12 senior leader review – including next steps and new ideas generation.	Opportunity for formalized line manager review and consolidation of learning, results, needs and ideas to feed into presentation to the senior management the following week.
12	Presentation to CEO or senior leader sponsor of objectives, actions, results, impact on business/people and next actions, new ideas and ongoing road map planning.	Consolidation of first 90 days' actions and initiation of forward plan for action and learning/support.

Figure 14c: *The 90-Day Roadmap, Weeks 9–12*

Weeks 9 and 10 are about getting on with the projects and tasks, a combination of doing and learning as the central themes. During Week 11, it's important to consider the effectiveness of all the activities in play, and to start to measure project or task impact, consolidating progress with stakeholders in preparation for a senior leader review at the end of the ninety days.

Week 11 is the opportunity for a review and consolidation of results, learning and ideas. This review should be done with the line manager and the project stakeholders at all levels and should feed into the presentation planning, preparation and practice in advance of the final week.

The focus of **Week 12** is the final presentation. This should be a high-stakes meeting during which candidates deliver an impactful presentation to the CEO or another senior leader, talking about objectives, actions taken, results secured and the impact on the business and people throughout the ninety days. The output focus isn't the presentation itself, but the preparation required to consolidate the results from the ninety days. This then leads to creating a new 90-Day Road Map with the next actions, new ideas, appropriate training, coaching and support. It's designed to be a stretch, but it's undertaken in a safe environment and supported by this comprehensive toolkit. It's an opportunity to fast-track learning and become a leader, no matter what your official role or level is.

The outputs for Weeks 9–12 are:

- Measurement of project or task impact and consolidation of progress with stakeholders

- Review and consolidation of results, learning and ideas

- Delivery of presentation for review at senior leadership meeting

- Creation of the next 90-Day Road Map

The Personal Development Mosaic

The Personal Development Mosaic supports the 90-Day Road Map for distributed leadership success. The Mosaic comprises select-and-incorporate menus of parallel learning and personal development interventions, which will build the necessary knowledge, skills and behaviors for all in-role CEOs to succeed and grow. Milvio DiBartolemeo reflects on how he's seen this kind of development contribute to enhanced impact:

> "[I have aimed] to become the blackbelt for guidance, with depth and breadth of knowledge and expertise across several domains, for people to bounce ideas around with. I now have a range of people, from work colleagues to social media contacts, seeking advice. With every role that I've held in my career, I've tried to learn everything about that role by investing in myself and undertaking related courses and

Knowledge	Behaviors	Leadership skills	Management skills	Personal skills	Organizational level support
Digital learning Internal videos Self-driven learning	Who models great leadership and management behaviors in your business – highlight what you can do and practice (from a personal, peer and management perspective)	Secure senior level mentor and specific training/learning action as defined with HR/talent liaison	One-to-one coaching from your line manager or most suited manager On-the-job observation	Interpersonal effectiveness – training provided by your company, eg communication, collaboration and EQ	Make leadership skills demonstration a part of performance measurement (www.artsprofessional.co.uk/magazine/article/leading-all-levels)
Time with leaders and managers to learn from them (mini interview/key success factors)	Sit with HR/talent manager and understand how values link to organization culture and the valued behaviors internally for the best individual contributors, managers and leaders	Online learning – eg LinkedIn Learning, Coursera, Open Sesame, Tigerhall A suitable mix of core skills, digital know-how and leadership/management skills	Project and project team management training and co-working with experienced PM to learn the ropes/secure tips, tricks and traps	Emotional intelligence assessment, learning and application	Reconnect employees to higher/wider purpose beyond job role – it is worth being/staying here (www.artsprofessional.co.uk/magazine/article/leading-all-levels)
Read articles/watch self-help videos on how to lead at any level in an organization	Feedback from manager and peers – what traits do they value you for and what would they advise you to do differently to step up?	Take the lead in projects with close support, feedback and coaching from your line manager or other manager – specifically around leadership KSBs	Interview a strong manager in the business for best practice advice (including HR perspective)	Team-building, development and performance training coaching / formal and informal feedback activity	Performance- and behavior-based recognition and reward pathway for stepping up "in role" (avoid career blockages and reward as broader contribution in role)

4Es self-assessment as a foundation stone to identify strengths, gaps and a development plan

Figure 15: *Personal Development Mosaic*

exams to become an authority in that subject matter. I've learned that influence will only get you so far; what's also required is positional authority."

As you can see below, there is a range of menus within the Mosaic, which cover knowledge, behaviors, leadership skills, management skills and personal skills. This is not exhaustive but provides a starting point to find the right personalized learning blend to move forward. This should be in place alongside the 90-Day Road Map, and beyond, to underpin in-role CEO success for those stepping in, stepping out or stepping up. The selection of learning interventions will look different for each person and provides plenty of ideas and concrete actions to take forward. No doubt it will also spark other ideas, which of course can be included in an expanded menu.

Let's look at an example of how it works. The first five menus are addressed to in-role CEOs themselves, alongside line management support. The sixth menu represents the parallel organizational suggestions, intended to reinforce the personal development activity of in-role CEOs.

Knowledge

Knowledge
Digital learning
Internal videos
Self-driven learning
Time with leaders and managers to learn from them (mini interview/key success factors)
Read articles/watch self-help videos on how to lead at any level in an organization

Digital learning is the first component of the knowledge menu. Self-driven learning could comprise watching educational videos to build your skillset, such as adopting remote working best practices, virtual collaboration and communication must-dos and so on. An in-role CEO has to be prepared to step up and seek out the resources that will give them the edge.

The second component is about figuring out how to spend more time with leaders and managers to learn from them first-hand. The third component is self-development through engaging with external resources. Some of the links at the end of this book would be a good place to start.

Behaviors

Below are some ideas for potential in-role CEOs to work through; these are behaviors that you can also model and cultivate.

Behaviors
Who models great leadership and management behaviors in your business – highlight what you can do and practice (from a personal, peer and management perspective)
Sit with HR/talent manager and understand how values link to organization culture and the valued behaviors internally for the best individual contributors, managers and leaders
Feedback from manager and peers – what traits do they value you for and what would they advise you to do differently to step up?

Leadership skills

The leadership menu looks specifically at leadership skillsets and where a potential in-role CEO can seek further advice, inputs and learning, such as having a mentor, attending training and driving their self-development.

Leadership skills
Secure senior level mentor and specific training/learning action as defined with HR/talent liaison
Online learning – eg LinkedIn Learning, Coursera, Open Sesame, Tigerhall
A suitable mix of core skills, digital know-how and leadership/management skills
Take the lead in projects with close support, feedback and coaching from your line manager or other manager – specifically around leadership KSBs

Management skills

The fourth menu moves from leadership (focusing on and doing the right things) to management skills – the how-to. How do we do things in the right way when working with, engaging and mobilizing others?

Management skills
One-to-one coaching from your line manager or most suited manager
On-the-job observation
Project and project team management training and co-working with experienced PM to learn the ropes/secure tips, tricks and traps
Interview a strong manager in the business for best practice advice (including HR perspective)

Personal skills

This menu considers the support for a personal skills suite to enhance those all-important interpersonal capabilities. These used to be called "soft skills", but as I have already mentioned, there is nothing soft about them. These are today's power skills to unlock relationships, collaborations, tough situations, team performance, networks and much more. Here we look at the personal effectiveness training to be provided by your company around (written and verbal) communication and collaboration, as well as things like presenting skills.

The other essential personal skill that we know sets great leaders apart from the merely "good" is emotional intelligence. In terms of training, an EQ assessment is key for the personal development of in-role CEOs. This can be done as part of training from a qualified line manager, or formal training undertaken by working with an emotional intelligence-certified practitioner. Emotional intelligence is such an important part of bringing out your inner CEO that I incorporate it into the support and development programs I design and deliver for organizations globally.

Personal skills
Interpersonal effectiveness – training provided by your company, eg communication, collaboration and EQ
Emotional intelligence assessment, learning and application
Team-building, development and performance training coaching / formal and informal feedback activity

Organizational input

This menu acknowledges the organization's responsibilities in supporting in-role CEOs as they embrace their developmental journey. This, mixed with the personal ownership of their learning, provides a robust, multi-strand approach to the support and development of people who are unleashing their inner CEO.

Organizational level support
Make leadership skills demonstration a part of performance measurement (www.artsprofessional.co.uk/magazine/article/leading-all-levels)
Reconnect employees to higher/wider purpose beyond job role – it is worth being/staying here (www.artsprofessional.co.uk/magazine/article/leading-all-levels)
Performance- and behavior-based recognition and reward pathway for stepping up "in role" (avoid career blockages and reward as broader contribution in role)

This Personal Development Mosaic is designed for in-role CEOs to work their way through the different components and create their personal development plan, strongly supported by the organization.

Some of this may be a little uncomfortable as people address where they need to improve their skills and confidence, but taking ownership of their self-development is a significant part of unleashing their inner CEO. Keep in mind that this is a menu of options. It's not essential to do all of it, but individuals can pick the things that are relevant to and right for them, based on their goals and the feedback they've received so far.

Together, the 4Es, 90-Day Road Map, thirty-six questions and the Personal Development Mosaic provide a powerful, practical toolkit for unleashing the inner CEO. As you can see, an organization must provide support, not only by creating the conditions for individuals to unleash their inner CEO but also through ongoing activities, leadership sponsorship, line manager support and a tailored personal development journey. In this new paradigm of the rapidly evolving future workplace, that journey should no longer be just about measuring the KPIs or objectives and key results (OKRs) for a specific job role. Managers must actively appreciate and recognize those stepping in, out and up and taking ownership of their development, in addition to delivering on the job.

The vision becomes more than just one of what the company is trying to achieve from a revenue generation point of view. It becomes an inspiring vision of possibility for everyone involved. It's about being awake to the broader purpose beyond individual job roles. As Michael Chavez and Sudanshu Palsule describe in their book, *Rehumanizing Leadership:*

> "Purpose is the life-force that runs through us and our organizations. The words we use to describe its presence are words like direction, passion, wellbeing, productivity, clarity, engagement and even joy. Organizations with a sense of purpose that goes beyond shareholder value are more productive and innovative."[29]

How can in-role CEOs start to operate in this new way of being? How can they support others to do so? By being enabled and empowered to lead with purpose, in a way that frees up their talent to innovate and excel, rather than limiting them to what they already do. We must all be encouraged to be more conscious of the ripple effect our actions have, not only on our customers but also on our colleagues and communities. It's essential to be aware of the social impact the organization has and to model the behaviors we'd like to see more of, both internally and externally.

This is the future of work, and that future is now. The toolkit outlined in this chapter provides extensive practical frameworks and everything that is needed to start putting all the elements in place. You can access more details, toolkits and templates at https://performanceworks.global/theinnerceo.

What next?

So far, we've looked at how to distribute leadership to in-role CEOs across the organization, and the strategic advantage that results from that. We've explored the rapid pace of change that is setting a context of continuous transformation, and why leaders and their organizations need to adapt. We've heard from several interviewees about the kind of mindset needed to establish a culture of distributed leadership. We've looked at the organizational structures that need to be in place (Chapter 3). In this chapter, we've seen that there is a negative as well as a positive side to the kind of empowerment we're aiming to embed, and I've given you a toolkit for realizing distributed leadership at all levels. In Chapter 5 we'll look at how you can safeguard your organization against the risks of unleashing distributed leadership and what happens when it goes wrong.

But first, my interview with Andrea Studlik explores how the upsurge in remote working has acceler- ated digital enablement and the need to support this through flatter structures of coaching, collaboration and communication. Andrea discusses how estab- lishing a safe environment is the responsibility of everyone in the organization, and how a robust infra- structure needs to support this.

Interview with Andrea Studlik

Andrea Studlik is a senior-level, global human capital expert, as well as a life and career coach, with expe- rience working across borders and cultures. Andrea was formerly senior director of talent management for Asia Pacific at JLL, and before that was director of learning and development and campus head at AXA University, Asia. This interview was recorded while Andrea was in post at JLL.

JEREMY: What does "leading at all levels" mean and why is it important in the workplace of the 2020s and beyond?

ANDREA: It's about the collaborative nature of work. All the stuff I'm working on now is project based. We work in multiple teams across multiple geog- raphies and we're all peers. We have to manage ourselves, our deliverables, our priorities and our stakeholders, once we get off the phone with each other. So, collaboration is more and more a critical skill.

JEREMY: So thinking about individual contributors who perhaps don't have that much experience, we have to also think about how to train them and model behaviors, don't we?

ANDREA: Exactly. I remember there was a project where we had more junior employees on the calls. Our expectation was that they would complete the tasks and deliver on schedule. So they had to take ownership to anticipate the expectations and requirements, dependent on what was happening, not only with people in their own office but also in various time zones and cultures and so on. There was a need for lateral thinking. That's hard to do.

So yes, we, as the more senior people, have a responsibility to help those who are stepping up to clarify goals, stay on track, create open feedback loops, have informal coaching moments and help them prioritize, so that they have a fighting chance of being successful and flourishing. We all have a responsibility in creating a culture whereby mutual help, peer and project team coaching and collaboration become the key ingredients for success. For everyone.

JEREMY: Is this a natural evolution of where organizations are going now, or is this a call for a revolution in how we work, collaborate and unleash the inner CEOs throughout organizations?

ANDREA: It has been largely evolutionary but perhaps some may need a mini revolution to accelerate it and formalize it. It's more important than ever to help people discover meaningful work. If we consider the situation right now, of those of us working from home, many are having trouble motivating themselves. They need to feel more connected to the work they are doing and to the people they are working with.

Remote working is developing new muscles to flex in all of us, and they need to be trained and toned up. So bold new rules of the road, collaborative ways of working and a more robust support infrastructure are needed in many organizations.

JEREMY: What's the benefit of empowering people who can step up at all levels, contributing beyond their job role, perhaps to something more strategic?

ANDREA: For those people, it's definitely accelerating their development. For example, when working on one or more projects, you don't just have your line manager, you're responsible to many people. Everybody has to own it. You have to keep yourself accountable to your own part of the project and in supporting others.

JEREMY: As all this comes together, what is the role of the line manager?

ANDREA: To me, it's very much like the saying, "It takes a village to raise a child." In the workplace, it takes this community to support one other, and a line manager to consolidate, provide clarity and make things come to life. I would argue that in new, flattened, more empowering structures it is the community that trumps the line manager in supporting, peer coaching and developing those unleashed inner CEOs.

For example, I have more interaction with some of my colleagues' team members than their line managers do, because they're supporting me and doing what I need done. So my feedback about their contribution, challenges, development areas and so on is required. I coach them informally. It really works. It's so cool.

JEREMY: What's in place for those individuals who step up in terms of self-development opportunities?

ANDREA: The Americas region is probably the furthest ahead just in terms of the number of development opportunities that they have at their disposal: not just training programs, but also conferences, job share and secondment opportunities. We are formalizing this across the other regions to support everyone who needs it. It's a key factor for successful empowerment across the company.

JEREMY: It's important to give everyone the tools and support they need.

ANDREA: Yes, it is. But the legacy challenge is that we have too much traditional learning delivery (face-to-face, etc). This is good, but we can make it more efficient with greater digitalization and mobile-based learning. Many companies are still locked into how they used to train and develop people, not changing the game around *what* needs to be developed, and how to best deliver the training, coaching and personal development.

JEREMY: What do you say to those who are resisting unleashing the inner CEOs within their people?

ANDREA: I think it's a really limiting belief, and maybe it's generational, maybe it's cultural, I don't know. These leaders may have a reinforcing internal dialogue: "In order for me to look good, I have to have a bunch of junior and less talented people below me." That's completely the opposite of what's true. When I think about all the greatest leaders I've known, it's because they showed vulnerability and they said, "I've got an amazing team who are better than me, because I don't know everything." And that makes them stronger.

JEREMY: Oh, it does. And then you are truly unleashing the power of the people, aren't you?

ANDREA: Exactly, because if that person has the confidence and the strength to just sit in that, admit that and be OK with that, it starts to make it OK for others to show that vulnerability as well because it's safe to do so. It's infectious and entirely positive.

JEREMY: What are the key enablers in organizations to unlock potential and give people permission to step up?

ANDREA: I think the first thing that comes to mind is self-confidence. When a person is self-confident then you can let go a little bit. You don't need to micromanage. Choose the best, make sure they're clear on what they need to do and then let them get on with it. Giving them space is a really important thing, but you also have to hold them accountable. It's like being a good parent.

And when I think about what I want to be doing in the next few years, I want to make sure that there are more companies that are thinking laterally or thinking without borders; that are hiring more independent workers on a much more frequent basis. We all know that a lot more people want to be working like this rather than as an employee. Again, it goes back to believing that you chose the right people, you gave them the right tools and the right vision, and now you let them get on with it.

FIVE

When Distributed Leadership Goes Wrong

In this chapter we're going to learn how to avoid the potential traps of distributed leadership, covering:

- The "ripple points" of when and how distributed leadership can go wrong, and how to prevent and correct this

- Case studies of empowerment going wrong – examples of overburdening and overreaching

- Balancing autonomy and support

Creating inner CEOs to make distributed leadership across our organization a reality is a radical and potentially disruptive act. It goes against the grain of twentieth-century vertical leadership structures where strategic decision-making was tightly grasped in the hands of a few senior leaders. If, as an organizational strategy, distributed leadership is not planned, executed and followed through, then it can be damaging. If the initiative fails, it will be even harder to try again in the future.

What a shame it would be if we made strong efforts to create the conditions for distributed leadership success, only to fail at the first or second hurdle by not following through with meaningful action at all levels. Thus, this chapter explores what can go wrong with distributed leadership and how it can be misunderstood or misaligned. I will give my tips for what to look out for at each stage of the process, as any missteps can have a ripple effect that can derail and disrupt the process when you should be focused on building momentum.

That said, should you identify some of the things we highlight in this chapter as going wrong or failing altogether in your organization, then everything we have covered in the book so far will enable you to quickly reposition, realign, reframe and refresh your approach going forward.

Great waves from tiny ripples grow

In any situation, process, strategy and plan, things can (and do) go wrong. What separates progress from regression or failure is so often the positive "can-do" mindset and spirit of those involved, where experimentation is valued as an opportunity for learning and refinement; and a focus on implementation success through momentum building and catching people doing it right. This all helps to build solid progress and the positive recognition of emerging new behaviors and actions at all levels, which is closely linked to culture building driven by enhanced shared values and beliefs.

There are a lot of moving parts to lead and manage – at the function level, at the team level, across management and our individual contributor population – and things can go wrong before they even get started. If the organization or senior leaders and management are not behind this agenda as a structural shift and as a radical new human capital framework, then nothing will happen. As the Dalai Lama said, "Just as ripples spread out when a single pebble is dropped into the water, the actions of individuals can have a far-reaching effect."[30]

As well as an individual not being bought in, wrong or misjudged implementation actions – or inaction – can lead to rapid failure. It is at the center of our organizations, like the pebble thrown into a pool, that our actions have the greatest ripple effect.

We have already covered the enablers of empowerment and transformation. In this chapter, I embrace the "single pebble" idea to highlight the greatest risks and biggest barriers to progress, the things that will lead to failure and, therefore, the priorities to get right from minute one. If you follow the guidelines in this book and live, breathe and champion positive action, this should be easy to do.

Below I list some of the early warning signs to look for and the corrective actions that will keep the implementation on track, improving and refining as you go, consistently across the organization. Understanding some of the bigger themes and what generally to watch out for will ensure strong oversight and meticulous management of the implementation and embedding of distributed leadership culturally across the organization. This is not an exhaustive list, and it will be even more robust when you add your own actions, red flags and advice to it.

Before we dive into this, let me reiterate that implementation failure is not the "fault" of the people. It is more often than not down to the first ripple point: the strategic, organizational conditions that may or may not be robust enough, and a lack of ongoing commitment and strong change mindset at the board, executive leadership and line manager levels.

Warning signs and corrective action

Things going wrong is not a disaster; often, mistakes are required for fast learning, refinement of the approach and steadier progress going forward. That said, if multiple things are going wrong at the same time, then the cumulative effect can be a big problem. The first ninety days of actions, measures and learning support that I listed earlier in the book ensure we get off to a strong start. It also helps us measure as we go, picking up on the more operational challenges that may emerge early in the process.

The good news is that the spirit of empowerment and the greater autonomy that is supporting our leaders at all levels provide the solid foundation you will need to adapt where needed and enable all-level communication and action. Everyone can be involved in the plan and should be acutely aware of the five main ripple points and what to watch out for; the process of oversight, feedback and wider communication; and how to adapt and take corrective action. This keeps things on track but doesn't overwhelm the few executive leaders and HR business partners who might have traditionally stepped in to steady the ship as small ripples became large waves. Now everyone can be part of the solution, from day one.

The Ripple Point model (Figure 16) highlights the most important aspects that lead to failure in distributed leadership. Each of the circles are "ripple points" as I call them. It is not exhaustive but represents the main areas of failure that I have observed across companies and public sector organizations I have worked with, particularly over the last three years since the release of the first edition of this book.

In the Ripple Point model, the closer to the center and the darker the circle is, the more likely it is that the inaction, wrong actions or poor behaviors will lead to rapid failure, and the more sharply that is felt by the rest of the organization, affecting engagement, motivation, mobilization and positive action. The opposite is also true. Recognizing these impacts is a huge step toward success and the ability to move forward with a stronger footing.

Words over actions
Strategic intent and first actions

1. Executive leadership mindset shift is not fully evident.
2. Organizational structure, guidelines, clarity and all-level buy-in not in place.
3. Talking the talk, not walking the walk.

Dangerous first steps

1. New measures, recognition and reward approach are not in place.
2. Line manager targeting shift to enable and guide all-level leadership is not consistent. This could lead to the rise of cliques, politics and potential failure.
3. Performance support orientation versus performance management is not in evidence.
4. No robust change management program in place to underpin the shift.
5. No parallel culture building to provide a solid foundation of new values and behaviors that will supercharge progress.
6. Lack of enabling digital technologies and ways of working to fast-track all-level autonomy, collaboration and communication.

Line management capability and momentum loss
Operational implementation and realities

1. Lack of alignment to organizational aims devalues the power of all-level efforts behind clear direction and goals.
2. Lack of momentum building – early wins evaporate as old habits and 'back to normal' mentality take over.
3. Working harder versus working smarter.
4. Balance is lost. Core job roles suffer as employees focus on other things.
5. Line managers are not skilled in coaching, guidance and enabling truly empowered teams and individuals.
6. Executive leaders not close enough to the overall organizational effort.

All-level effectiveness and empowerment roadblocks

1. New learning and development infrastructure is not solid enough and does not provide the skills building quick enough to support in-role CEOs.
2. Lack of communication glue across the organization.
3. Too many different projects being initiated but not fully followed through or measured and reported on.
4. Inadequate feedback loops and resulting action.
5. Spirit of experimentation is not encouraged.
6. Trust issues start to take root and can impact culture-building efforts.

Managing ongoing growing pains

1. Rise of those embracing their newfound empowerment and those riding the wave of others.
2. New ideas, innovations and efforts not being formally curated and embedded across the organization.
3. Data not being used from day one to measure progress, refine actions and make decisions.
4. Frustrations and inconsistencies becoming more evident.
5. Rigidity versus flexibility in the way people work, communicate and collaborate.
6. Ongoing change management to recognize enablers and barriers to success evaporates.

Figure 16: *The Ripple Point model*

In each of the five ripple point discussions below there is advice for what to prioritize – ie, the things that are most important to get right – and traps that need to be avoided at all costs as, more often than not, they lead to failure, a reinstated hierarchy and even less flexibility as an organization than existed before. This is the negative side of empowerment that we want to avoid.

Ripple Point 1: Words over actions

When any drive to empower others goes wrong, the top is where we need to look first for the cause. With the best intent at organization level, if we aren't seeing the implementation and changes in behaviors, we should look at what is being modeled by the senior leaders and, often, the executive board. Are senior-most leaders and managers changing themselves? Are they walking the walk? Below, two in-role CEOs describe some of the factors that contribute to failure at this level:

> "Bottom-to-top leadership mentality, lack of presence from the executive level and retaining/hiring leaders who talk the walk, or never walk the talk."
> — Rasie Bamigbade, in-role CEO

> "If you're led to believe there's progress and there isn't, then you don't work in an empowered way anymore."
> — Ehecatl Hunt-Duarte, in-role CEO

The symptoms manifesting from a lack of implementation momentum at executive leadership level can be summarized as:

- Words over actions

- Intention to change without a concerted effort to change

- A refusal to break down hierarchical barriers and introduce newer methods like horizontal management principles

- An immobilization at leadership and line management levels; as first actionable steps, guidelines and supporting structures have not been thought through or owned

- A lack of ownership in HR, who have not been suitably empowered to make this happen with the strong endorsement of the C-suite

This first ripple is the most powerful, in both positive and negative terms. When empowerment is handled with care and commitment, the foundation is solid and progress, in implementation terms, can be rapid. When it is not, it becomes words over actions and there is a real risk of failure before we even begin, as the employee sentiment is, "Here we go again. We have heard it all before and it didn't happen, so it won't happen now." I am sure many of you reading this will be familiar with that experience.

This is why this first ripple point is the most powerful and damaging and can drive failure before anything has even got started, from day one. Executive leaders and all levels of management should be acutely aware of how they could be the drivers of outright failure or success supported (or not) by a formalized reimagining of the organizational structure in systemic terms.

To avoid this trap, below are some suggestions for where to look for help in this book and what to be mindful of:

- Be ready. Create the conditions for success upfront. Don't try to retrofit when things start going wrong. You could do more damage than good.

- See Chapter 2. To "be ready", you should compete the Five Point Star assessment for overall organizational readiness, ideally at executive leadership level, including HR and human capital leaders.

- See Chapter 3. Be mindful of what needs to be in place before any major announcements or actions.

- Once you are sure of readiness at executive leadership and across management, and that there has been a consideration of how to restructure management levels and supporting mechanisms (if required), you can move step by step through the next stages.

- Be aware of the ripple points ahead of you as the launch gets underway. Ensure there is a leadership and management steering group that acts as the "governance" body – like an empowerment board.

- Keep a close eye on progress through the 90-Day Road Map, the weekly recommended measures (and those you add), and the associated learning boost across the organization to build the knowledge, skills and behaviors that will magnify distributed leadership action and impact.

- Finally, leaders need to be doers, not casual observers talking the talk. This is meaningless and can come across as apathy at best and arrogance at worst.

This list is just a starting point. Make your own list of what you would add to arm yourself with further safeguards.

The next ripple point, which can also lead to rapid failure (or accelerated progress when done right) concerns the supporting structures, processes and systems to fortify distributed leadership. This is where people, process and technology either strengthen implementation resolve and success, ensuring that each element is "fit for purpose" and will enable the movement to distributed leadership, or act as a barrier to it. When this goes wrong, we see processes that haven't evolved to support the new approach; people who are not bought in to the process or aware of what they need to do differently; and supporting technology that overwhelms the effort rather than boosts it, it or is simply not right for what it is intended to do. A robust change management program will strengthen implementation success; without it, rapid failure will most likely follow. It's all part of the execution planning, communication and wider engagement strategy. Change management is an important parallel to culture building in implementation success terms.

The role of leaders, and especially implementing managers, in this brave new world, needs careful consideration, planning and explanation, as they remain an important part of momentum building at this stage. If the structural components from the first ripple above do not lead to an evolved management approach, then old habits will persist and new habits will have no chance to embed. The shift in management mindset and approach is moving away from supervision toward guidance, coaching and support, which enables individuals to embrace a more autonomous working existence by stepping in, stepping out or stepping up. Without managers helping to create early wins and actively celebrating small steps taken, initial successes and the new, emerging role models, efforts could evaporate. Just as easily, efforts can be reinforced and galvanized with the right approach.

This powerful ripple point remains largely strategic as the initial implementation is bolstered by supporting systems, structure, new processes, expectations and ways of operating (at all levels). Clarity of communication becomes paramount; without it, there will be a lot of frustrated people across the organization, waiting for direction, delivery on the empowerment promise, or simply for something – in fact, anything – to happen. Tim Lupinacci says,

> "Changing people's minds that 'this time we will really do it' comes with increased skepticism, increased objections and often without the energy you really need to get everyone involved and fired up to launch that rocket ship."

This connects directly to the first ripple point, which can magnify the negative impact of this second point if things have not been led effectively from the start. Conversely, it can ripple out more positively and – importantly – quickly, when things kick off in the right way, with a huge boost from the executive and management.

Again, I have some suggestions for where to look for help in this book and what to be mindful of in avoiding this trap:

- See Chapter 3 on supercharging organizational progress. You need a strong focus on the change management plan. There is a lot of change. Don't underestimate the need for a strong hand leading this internally; this remains part of your "empowerment governance".

- Work will need to have been done to consider what organizational values, beliefs and behaviors will be most suited to distributed leadership. This work will strengthen culture building and foster a sense of belonging for those remote workers, highly valued independent workers, part-timers and other stakeholders who will contribute to the overall success of the organization, alongside the core of your permanent workforce.

- An important factor for success is the digital ecosystem you put in place to enable seamless, easy collaboration, communication, reporting, recognition (including badges and awards if you're using them) and open feedback loops for sharing, flagging issues and all-level contribution to the ongoing success.

- Ensure the strategic ripple points are locked down, validated and signed off by the empowerment governance board (if you have one), before moving into the operational reality. The ingredients for success will all be in place and the whole internal movement will be easier.

Think about what you would add to arm yourself with further safeguards.

Ripple Point 3: Line management capability and momentum loss

Our third ripple point is at the intersection of our distributed leadership execution, the point at which strategic actions are completed and operational execution begins. On the positive side, if the other two points have been managed well, we will be making good progress. Yet each stage in the journey has its challenges as well as its opportunities, and as we get into the more operational elements of making distributed leadership a reality, we must keep a close eye on progress, as we may need to adapt to how things are going on the ground, and within the hearts and minds of managers and employees. This is a dangerous point in our implementation: we do not want to waste the strong strategic focus and actions, by failing when we get into the implementation itself.

There are so many moving parts that things can be lost in a sea of action and different approaches. One of the clients I worked with in North and Latin America had appointed a brand-new CoE – chief of empowerment. They realized that no single leader at executive level was owning the process, and that to formalize what had become one of the biggest structural shifts in their recent history, an accountable leader was needed. Therefore, a new leadership role was created, with a new structure underneath them, to enable the whole process, with appropriate measures of success at both strategic and operational levels. Managers were working with the CoE whose roles were 100% focused on supporting all levels of management in the business as a "best practice hub" for sharing new best line manager practices and learnings, as a community-based approach. It worked like a dream and brought all the moving parts across this third ripple point – and others – together under one roof. It accelerated implementation two-fold (according to the CEO) and fast-tracked positive results (also according to the same, now happy CEO!).

As we move into the operational implementation, we multiply the moving parts. If there are persistent issues from the steps before; if things have not been structured for success; if there is a lack of consistent roll-out and management approach; or a lack of clear communication with clarity of the why, what and how, then we have a major failure risk.

Before I provide some tips for making meaningful operational progress, you must take a minute to understand the true scale of your activity (dependent on whether you are a small, medium or large organization or institution). It must be acknowledged that this is a sea change for everyone. An obvious but often overlooked decision is to "slow down to speed up" in operational terms. There is no compulsion to make it an "everywhere, everyone, anywhere" play from the get-go. Do a pilot; be selective, secure data, refine the plan and create champions at all levels to help you take the message and actions out to the wider organization.

Below are my suggestions for where to look for help in this book and what to be mindful of to avoid the traps at this stage:

- If you have done a mini or medium-level pilot and have refined your approach, or if you are ready to go, then Chapter 4 is your blueprint for starting the operational stage in the right way. The 4Es assessment will help to establish a benchmark for where your people are now, where they are heading and the most appropriate supporting plan for helping them achieve their aims, thus fueling the overall growth engine of the business. The assessment and associated individual discussions will also help to establish preferences and competency to step in, step out or step up, as discussed in Chapter 2.

- Your next safeguard is the 90-Day Road Map (see Chapter 4), completed at the organizational level, by business unit if required, as well as individually, regardless of level, role, location or designation. Then, linking these actions to the weekly measures and a parallel learning track going forward will allow for regular temperature checks, open communication lines, early detection of best practices and risks and consistent adaptation across the organization. This will keep everyone aware and on top of what is happening and where.

- Importantly we must look after the whole person, not just the employee in a role. Wellbeing and emotional engagement, as part of the distributed leadership intent, will be good measures of success or otherwise. My model, the Six Centers of Me (see Chapter 6) will enable any individual, at any level, to self-assess, share and discuss as appropriate.

Think about what you would add to the above to arm yourself with further safeguards.

Ripple Point 4: All-level effectiveness and empowerment roadblocks

The fourth ripple point concerns all-level operational effectiveness and emerging roadblocks that could start to eat into the spirit of empowerment.

Empowering others doesn't just happen. Offering greater autonomy for employees to think, act and do differently requires careful planning and management. Distributed leadership at all levels will fail if organizations do not build the new knowledge, skills and behaviors required to be a leader at any level. This comes with a need for budget, resourcing and total commitment from leaders and managers to dramatically shift the organizational skills bench. Without this, we risk "headless chickens" running around our organization, occasionally hitting the mark, but most likely doing damage, negatively impacting others and potentially failing in all aspects of their role, not just the task at hand.

Consider: everyone is excited. They embrace greater autonomy. They want to contribute beyond the job role and they have lots of ideas. However, if this is not handled carefully or is not managed to ensure some level of organizational grip alongside that individual energy, then things could rapidly spiral out of hand. For example, there can be too much management reliance on the most motivated and capable team members.

Of course, we want to see inner CEOs taking positive ownership of their new autonomy and emerging as strong leaders at their level. However, if executive leaders and managers are not careful, then this could lead to overburdening the individuals concerned and potentially setting them up for under-productivity, increased working hours, exhaustion or, worse, burnout. Line managers in these situations have a particular responsibility to take steps to avoid this and rapidly identify if it is happening. It does happen all too often in the workplace, as the first case study below demonstrates – an actual situation that led to a highly unsatisfactory result for everyone.

The positive step of empowering this person can also move into negative territory if their autonomous working is allowed to get out of control, with empowered people feeling they can do anything and taking on too much, increasingly operating without reference to their supporting line manager and, in extreme cases, "going rogue". Think about the recent history of rogue traders, political supporters living on the extremes of their beliefs and operators in our businesses doing what they want, when they want. The two specific risks associated with this are:

- No oversight to qualify ideas and actions

- Potential loss of alignment to organizational aims

Executive leaders and line managers must be aware of this and acknowledge that it could happen. The second case study below highlights a real example.

The risk is ever-present, so a central part of the new role of executive leaders and managers is to support, guide, qualify and collaborate across the business to ensure that greater autonomy does not equate to losing overall control. If this starts to happen, then another risk is raised: the re-emergence of over-control, micro-management and hierarchical influence. This will lead to a regression, not progress; and to old habits, not new ways of operating; bad culture (in the worst case), not good culture.

Ripple effects can be individually manageable without any significant impact but could quickly run into dangerous territory if multiple breaks in the system were to emerge and persist. There is a strong onus on our line managers, team leaders, functional heads and project leads – as much as our unleashed inner CEOs – because the process and momentum still have to be managed in a traditional sense, as well as supported in line with the spirit of the change.

Where to look for help in this book and what to be mindful of:

- Chapter 4 onwards is our main guidance system for managing this ripple point while revisiting Chapter 3 to sense-check the organizational components. As mentioned above, creating a line of accountability through, for example, a CoE, and a new business unit to support the move to a model of distributed leadership helps mitigate much of this risk.

- HR business partners have a critical role to play in ensuring the supporting pillars of success are built and remain strong – whether that be training, coaching, data capture, regular feedback loops and so on. See Chapters 2 and 4 for ways to create pathways for in-role CEOs that have clear goals and structures.

- This stage may require a dose of courage for those in more senior positions, and especially for line managers, as they adopt new ways of managing, supporting and communicating with their teams. Letting go can be the hardest thing, particularly as the spirit of experimentation, learning from early failures and mistakes becomes more embedded. This is all about managing the growing pains (see the next ripple point) but also requires the positive mindset discussed in Chapter 3.

Think about what you would add to arm yourself with further safeguards.

Ripple Point 5: Managing ongoing growing pains (and the old habits that are dying hard)

The fifth ripple refers to what can happen in the medium to long term once implementation has been successful and the cultural DNA of the organization enables strong autonomy at all levels and distributed leadership is a reality. How do we keep building momentum? How do we adopt evolving best practices? How do we maintain leadership and management oversight, while living the spirit and reality of distributed leadership? How do we adapt, support and capture relevant data to help us adapt our approach? It is easy for the organization to slow down at this point. Consolidation is, of course, key as we unleash our inner CEOs, but cannot be at the expense of progress when speed is most likely the competitive currency for your business.

We established early on in this book that not everyone will embrace being empowered in the same way. Some will "step in", some will want to "step out" and some will grab hold of the opportunity to "step up". There may be others who will cruise through, riding on the coattails of their colleagues and not contributing in ways that fit the spirit of greater autonomy. This is where productivity could be lost, both from those non-contributors and from others who are picking up their slack.

It may be that the organization is not experiencing the kind of results or impact expected. Perhaps projects are starting to overrun; maybe we are not qualifying ideas or managing innovation at all levels effectively. This is as much a management issue as one concerning individual contributors. It can lead to "panic mode" and could risk regression to old-style management practices and short-termism. This is bound to happen at some point. Practices across the business can be inconsistent, with different management styles and preferences, trumping the aligned organizational approach that leaders and managers should aspire to. If this is allowed to become widespread, the whole system gets more rigid. A lot of progress can be destroyed in a short period if we are not careful. This is about awareness and proactive action-taking.

Finally, it may simply be that the organization has experienced some churn. There are new managers in role, new leadership and new individual contributors. If they have not been onboarded in the right way and given a clear picture of what they were stepping into, then individual preferences and styles can emerge, leading to greater inconsistencies both horizontally and vertically. Rasie Bamigbade reflects on her experiences of inconsistent and even chaotic implementation in organizations and the negative outcomes of this:

> "Being a high-performing leader and using my voice effectively came at a cost. I was promised one project or another role one year after the other at different organizations. When I was ready and had completed my plan of action, I was told to do something else on two different occasions and for two different companies."

To avoid this, HR should own the whole process from the start, factoring in the need to communicate externally as strongly as internally around the culture, structure and spirit of the organization and how it operates. There should be no surprises and new people in new roles should own the responsibility to build on, not eat into, the progress that has been made.

By now, distributed leadership is largely "the way we operate". Of course, no organization will be able to claim that it is a "root to branch" shift. There will still be old habits, apathy, cruisers, short-term issues and the usual day-to-day challenges and opportunities. Largely, we can accept this as the reality of what we are doing, with the majority making a huge positive difference to the organization and gradually "infecting" the more negative or apathetic voices to at least think differently for a moment, rather than the other way around.

But as the old saying goes, "old habits die hard". Management must be mindful of this, and so too should peer leaders at all levels, whether they are stepping in, stepping out or stepping up.

Where to look for help in this book and what to be mindful of:

- Keep a close focus on the measures in place across and then beyond the 90-Day Road Map described in Chapter 4. There is an opportunity in Week 9 or 10 of the Road Map to create a working group that can establish the next ninety days, or the next 180 days, creating new milestones, weekly measures and supporting activities, based on learnings from experiences so far. This is a great opportunity for an all-level working group, supported by the empowerment governance board (if you have one), or by strategic and operational steering groups.

- Look out for the emergence of workplace politics and cliques and have a plan to deal with them.

- You can revisit Chapter 3 and Chapter 4 for guidance and critical questions to ask across each of the 4Es to help identify issues or opportunities and find mutually agreed ways forward, supported by on-the-job coaching guidance. This will support your own discussions and thoughts, helping you to identify, tackle and solve any issues in a manner that reflects the spirit of empowered working and our unleashed in-role CEOs.

- Look externally for other practices and create sharing networks internally and externally.

- Bring in the voice of the customer to demonstrate how the internal move has step-changed customer-centricity and the expanded customer journeys you could be transforming.

Think about what you would add to arm yourself with further safeguards.

An important element of genuine distributed leadership is the improvements it generates across diversity, equity and inclusion. This is central for leaders in today's organizations, as it is at the heart of environmental and social governance expectations. If empowerment is not consistent, if some are excluded or treated unfairly, and if a diversity of thinking is not embraced, then it can not only lead to a failure of distributed leadership but to a collapse of diversity, equity and inclusion progress – this is dangerous ground for any company in the modern era. This is something Rasie Bamigbade experienced first-hand:

"When I wasn't promoted and another manager was hired externally, my teams asked questions. When this manager was underperforming and not responding to the needs of our team, it made things even more challenging."

One area where a fine balance needs to be struck in driving a culture of distributed leadership is the balance of autonomy and support. The degree of autonomy needs to be aligned with an appropriate level of support for each individual, taking into account their starting point. There is no one-size-fits-all approach here. Too little in the way of support structures and guidance can mean individuals are ill-equipped to lead confidently. Too much can stifle leadership before it's even begun. To illustrate these points, I share below two case studies of people I have worked with (names have been changed).

Case study 1: Overburdening top performers

Rick was a successful project manager in a small team, working in a university. He was well liked and regarded as the "glue" in the team, being the most experienced and long-serving employee.

One of the team leaders in another part of the university, Anushka, left quite suddenly on long-term sick leave. Sue, the director, said that she wanted to give more opportunities to other employees to "act up" and expand their role experience. She suggested that Rick cover the role while Anushka was off sick, reassuring him that she would provide him with daily catch-up calls. Because Rick was already at the top of his pay grade, the new role wouldn't offer much in the way of financial reward, but he was looking for a challenge and to develop his skills so he decided to accept the temporary role.

Due to Anushka's sudden departure, there wasn't much of a handover, so Sue organized weekly meetings with Rick's previous line manager. She gave Rick lots of advice about how he should manage his day and his time. Even so, it proved to be a lot to take on, and at the end of one of their calls, Sue expressed concern about the productivity of the team and started to challenge Rick on this. He was taken aback, telling us during the interview that he was under far more pressure than he had expected, taking on all aspects of Anushka's role. He was further concerned that there was no clear indication that Anushka would actually return. This was more pressure than he had signed up for. Nevertheless, he decided to keep his head down and do his best.

On their next call, Rick received even worse news from Sue, who explained that her boss was unhappy with the team's performance and that the team would need to be restructured if Rick was unable to up the productivity. Yet Rick himself would be given no further support, training or coaching to help him through the "part-time" team leadership role. Rick, more worried at this point for the team, focused on how he could help boost their productivity. He ended up working longer hours on operational tasks because people's jobs were on the line, but it paid off and the team started to deliver better results. Rick told me that while he felt overwhelmed, this was a real energizer for him. Until he met with Sue again.

In the next meeting, Sue dropped the news that the team was being restructured anyway, and that most of them would be offered the opportunity to transfer to a different team. Rick said that he had protested strongly at this news, and then was told that the changes had already been decided – without any communication with or involvement from him. Sue simply told him that he would now have to work with the HR business partner.

At this stage of the interview, I could tell Rick was getting agitated. He told me that he had started to suffer from stress and burnout due to the long days and the strain of trying to keep team morale up. He felt resentful that he had been burdened with this difficult task when what he'd been expecting was a development opportunity: to be an empowered team leader with the support of his leader and line managers. This didn't happen and, not long after Anushka returned, Rick decided that he didn't want to progress in this organization. He started to look for a new role outside the university, which he duly secured, and he is now much happier and more fulfilled in his current organization.

What went wrong?

Looking back at our ripple points to identify the issues at play here, Rick's empowerment was ad hoc. There appears to have been no executive leadership support; the line manager reverted to a supervisory function and was clearly not prepared to support this kind of empowerment. She certainly did not understand the conditions needed to provide the more meaningful support that was required, nor her responsibility to be actively involved, as opposed to just filling a gap and getting on with her own priorities. As things started to go wrong, blame came into play as short-term needs overcame the longer-term progress that Rick had started to make.

This was a recipe for failure, with the true intent – to fill a gap and put someone in a position to play team leader – all too clear. This was not Rick's fault or ultimate responsibility, but Sue's. The result? The best performer, a widely respected member of the faculty, became disillusioned, burned out and unhappy, to the extent that he simply left. This was a completely avoidable outcome. Internally, the result was angry colleagues (the previous team members) with more distrust of leadership and the university, leaving more work to do for leaders and managers like Sue.

Case study 2: An individual contributor "going rogue" in a financial services scale-up

An interview with a head of HR provided a cautionary tale. It concerns both overreaching by the empowered employee and a loss or lack of oversight from the line manager and the manager's manager. In this case, empowerment became a free-for-all, and that is not good for anyone, being potentially damaging internally and in the eyes of customers.

A high performer, Rachel, embraced the spirit of empowerment, making early progress and enjoying being so fulfilled in her job. She was on top of her core job role but was excited by the new opportunities and autonomy. Rachel's line manager, Manish, with the best intent, let her run with it. In a short time, Rachel was involved in many parts of the business, often without Manish's prior knowledge. She became convinced of her own ability to drive the business forward. She was certainly capable but did not have the nuanced communication, interpersonal skills and even leadership skills she needed. Opinions on Rachel started to polarize and two specific issues were flagged to HR.

When our interviewee, the head of HR, got to hear about it, she analyzed the information being provided. Rachel, it seems, was busy doing things that were not sanctioned, not always appropriate or aligned to organizational objectives and were creating tensions in her team, function and more broadly. It was overreaching on a scale that HR had not anticipated.

What went wrong?

When I asked where the accountability for the situation lay, the head of HR pointed the finger at Rachel's line manager, Manish. Undoubtedly Manish was accountable up to a point, but I challenged that HR did not have enough oversight, exposing a big "miss" in the process: the lack of clear guidelines, expectations and support mechanisms. It was quite a sobering discussion for the head of HR. The bigger issue this exposed was that there were large inconsistencies in how distributed leadership was being implemented and even greater discrepancies in the understanding of what more autonomy at all levels looked like.

I was able to work closely with HR and the sponsoring executive leadership members and we recaptured the initiative. Situations can be rescued; new plans and processes can be implemented. It's not failure – it's learning.

Balancing autonomy and support

As the above case study demonstrates, we want to avoid empowerment becoming "too much of a good thing" in terms of allowing individuals to "go rogue". It's important to have the right level of management to offer support, guidance, correction, recognition and encouragement within the boundaries of strategic intent. This requires the right balance of autonomy and support.

A 2016 study by Cheong and colleagues[31] went deeper into why empowerment can both enhance performance (enable) and also have a negative influence (burdening). The researchers identified leadership behaviors that contribute to self-efficacy, such as emotional support, words of encouragement and models of success with which people can identify and experience proficiency. They also found that certain empowering behaviors of leaders can sometimes result in reduced motivation and performance since they burden "followers" without adequately resourcing them. This burdening effect of empowerment could be caused by job-induced tension, such as lack of clarity over roles, cognitive burden due to task-switching and a perception that the leader is abdicating their responsibilities.

The researchers concluded: "It is crucial for managers to remember that empowering leadership has its own limits and to be realistic when they use empowering leadership to achieve the most positive effects," and that, "In particular, leaders should consider followers' traits and situational factors when they engage in empowering behaviors towards followers."[32]

As with the ripple points described earlier in the chapter, ongoing monitoring and reflection are important at all levels to flag when empowerment may be burdensome or lead to other unintended consequences. In essence, flexibility in style and approach is as important as a dose of courage to allow for great experimentation and effective oversight of the new situations that may arise (such as in how individuals are collaborating, how decisions are being made, what data is being used to inform progress and so on).

Empowerment is about unlocking a spirit of experimentation, among other things, in the organization itself. It isn't all going to go right, which is why milestones, regular feedback, check-in steps and measures need to be in place and managed. Clarity of communication and intent is paramount, for which oversight is required. Empowerment and distributed leadership don't remove the need for some kind of hierarchical system. We still need strategic leaders and managers to make decisions. We need to manage, measure and secure results. The intent is more to grow the organizational skills and will to unleash the power of the many, positively, and take a more collective approach to organizational growth.

What next?

In the next chapter, I'll guide you through the personal component, which builds on the organizational foundation. First, though, we have another interview, this time with human capital and talent professional Emma Saxby.

Emma's interview acts as a convenient bridge between the organizational and the personal. She is passionate about unlocking the power within our employee population; to do this, we must have the organizational conditions and structures in place before we can empower our people to step up and achieve great things.

Following the interview with Emma, I have added a brand-new interview with James Cross. Now design director for Duke Corporate Education, and an ex-commander in the British Army, James brings an organization-level perspective, exploring both the positive and negative sides of unleashing empowerment in high-stakes environments such as the military.

Interview with Emma Saxby

Emma Saxby has spent the last twelve years in the world of HR, in various roles. She started in learning and development, moved into talent management and then focused on senior-level executive development, leadership pipelines and graduate development. Emma has worked for large multinationals such as AXA Insurance and DSM, the purpose-led sciences company. She recently founded her own coaching business, operating across Asia Pacific, the UK and Europe.

In this interview, she puts line management under the spotlight, explaining how it must shift from a traditional supervisory role to one of empowerment, and how cross-functional and multi-project work can enable new possibilities.

JEREMY: What impact can companies expect if they unleash the inner CEOs at every level in their organizations?

EMMA: Having leaders who are enlightened and mentally ready accelerates transformation and reduces the need for continual short-term restructuring attempts. On the other hand, losing sight of the long term can mean slipping into "old ways" of leading, managing and supervising, which doesn't encourage empowerment or employee engagement.

JEREMY: In the companies you have worked for, how have the more enlightened leaders created the conditions and environment that unleash our inner CEOs?

EMMA: They invest in the younger generation to accelerate their development and allow them to contribute beyond their job role, early in their career. This is motivating and engaging for new, young employees. They also invest in upskilling the rest of their organizational population, which helps to introduce the desired cultural shifts and environment so that everyone feels they can contribute strategically and operationally to the business. In my experience, the companies that do this well have a strong link between company leadership and HR leadership.

JEREMY: For some companies, there is a lot of trial and error. How relevant is the mantra of failing fast, often and early for these transforming companies?

EMMA: Very. We do see evidence of early success in some of these businesses. It's because they create a space and an environment where people can test, feel empowered and upskill simultaneously.

Unfortunately, in some companies, the leaders don't model behaviors, HR does not own its message and no one champions the cause. Therefore, it becomes too risky for individual contributors to step up, experiment, fail, learn and take greater ownership.

JEREMY: You mentioned removing layers in the business. What is the role of the line managers, and how do you mobilize and engage them in managing differently?

EMMA: This is the most crucial part. Managers will need to be repurposed and reskilled to be coaches, guides and collaborators for growth. By doing this, you will engage a hugely important part of the population who will be the fuel behind unleashing the inner CEOs.

This needs to become a part of the company's DNA. It's a cultural shift underpinned by new values that accelerate the ability to take ownership at every level in the organization, supported by amazing coaches who become the catalysts for unleashing the inner CEOs of our best and brightest. My advice is to make empowering your teams a part of your structure and process.

JEREMY: How does this manifest itself in how work gets done, as we move into a truly empowered state of unleashed inner CEOs and repurposed line managers?

EMMA: In my experience, it accelerates companies becoming more project-focused, led by cross-functional teams who are empowered to own the objective and work together for successful implementation. Rather than pigeon-holing our people, we see a holistic, longer-term contribution. This transcends roles and takes people down a path they can grow on, by being involved in different projects across many parts of the business, rather than being locked into one linear route and role. It's far more motivating and, ultimately, a more productive way of working.

JEREMY: In terms of the broader implications for organizations on this trajectory, how does it impact the way we should attract, recruit, develop, retain and grow an increasingly valuable human capital pool?

EMMA: As an HR professional, I'd say, "You can come into this organization, we will invest our time and energy in developing you, but we're also going to strengthen your strengths, and give you flexibility around the things that you need to be able to contribute, far beyond your job role."

It's all about having a more flexible approach to HR and human capital management so that it meets people's individual needs, instead of a collective one-size-fits-all approach. But a lot of companies don't follow through by delivering on their promises, and it doesn't take long for people to react. "Whoa, this is not at all what you sold me. This is what we discussed, and this is nowhere near where we are." If you're going to create an environment that embraces a flexible, new way to deal with human resources, you have to believe it and you have to systematically deliver on your promises. Otherwise, you'll lose people to competitors who are doing it well. You'll find it harder to attract new talent, as your employer branding reputation will suffer and, in the digital world, that can quickly go viral.

JEREMY: What would you put in place to build momentum and continue to support the people who are taking ownership to unleash their inner CEOs?

EMMA: I'd set up a buddy system in parallel with the supporting elements we've already covered. Peer support is something that is often missed but is helpful when you have a flatter, more interdependent, collaborative culture. Whether you're an executive, a CEO or a graduate, you pair up with a buddy, somebody who supports you, helps you practice for meetings or presentations, and offers mutual coaching support.

There's an exercise I've done many times in training sessions. You ask people, "What is it that you admired about a leader who had an impact on you?" I love listening to the answers. You get the most beautiful responses from people – real, raw responses – and that's what I see as "self-leadership". It's the things they admire that help them to develop and strive to be better than they are, that challenge them and help them get comfortable with being uncomfortable. That's them starting their journey to unleash their own leadership, their inner CEO.

Interview with James Cross

As a design director at Duke Corporate Education, James assists with the design and delivery of innovative developmental and educational solutions for a variety of global clients. Before joining Duke CE, James served as an officer in the British Army for over sixteen years. He has undertaken six operational tours in Northern Ireland, Kosovo, Sierra Leone, Iraq and, most recently, Afghanistan, before transitioning into financial services for five years.

JEREMY: What, in your experience, can corporate enterprise learn from the armed forces, in terms of building a culture of empowerment?

JAMES: Fundamentally, we have a "mission command" philosophy in the military. What that means is empowering your people to execute whatever the unifying purpose is, or the commander's intent. This philosophy needs to run through the entire organization. I believe this comes down to four key factors: communication, initiative, example and loyalty.

In terms of communication, whether at the top of the chain or the bottom, you should be spending 60–70% of your time ensuring that that message gets through, so there's no confusion about what you have to achieve. You're not telling people how to achieve it; you're leaving that up to their ingenuity.

There's also a personal responsibility, if you are a subordinate, that if you have any doubt in your mind, to be questioning. So it's a two-way relationship. You've got to engender a culture of initiative, so your people can seize on fleeting opportunities as they present themselves.

The third thing is example. Every leader has to embody those examples; you have to be doing what you say. By doing that you create confidence in people, whether that's the highest standards of execution, integrity or moral courage.

The final thing is loyalty. This isn't loyalty as blind obedience; it goes both ways. The senior commander must be loyal to their people – they're not going to expose them to undue risk without consideration – but also, all people have loyalty to those beside, below and above them.

JEREMY: What was your impression when you left the military and you walked through the corporate doors for the first time and observed leadership in that environment?

JAMES: I found that it was hierarchical; people were very much within their swim lanes, and they didn't step out of them. It just struck me that people weren't being used to their full potential.

JEREMY: What were the specific situations where you found that the armed forces as a whole, or your company, benefited from empowered people at all levels?

JAMES: I think, for me, the most challenging tour was Afghanistan. You really have to trust your subordinates to be able to make decisions and do things, because they're going to have to.

And sometimes you can control that – in Afghanistan especially it was very tempting to do so, because you have things like live video feeds, right down to soldier level. But actually, that's the thing you have to resist. Just because you can control, doesn't mean you should be controlling – you could end up smothering initiative and stifling the tempo and agility.

JEREMY: It's interesting to me that leaders and commanders within the armed forces really buy into this from a mindset point of view, first of all, but also understand the clear benefits of doing that from a broader, distributed leadership perspective. Was that your own experience of being in command of a unit?

JAMES: Very much so, because it also comes down to confidence in yourself and self-awareness, both of your strengths and your weaknesses, and being comfortable first of all with ambiguity, and second, knowing that you don't have all the answers.

In times of real pressure, I actually felt a sense of calm, because I knew that it wasn't all on me. I had to compute it all and bring it together and give direction, but there were lots of other capable people who could help me to do that. And I think the key thing there is humility.

JEREMY: When you say "it's not all on me," that's not a mindset that I see much of in the corporate space. Why do you think that is?

JAMES: Because fundamentally, it comes with risk. And it's hard work because everyone will have their strengths and be at different levels of development. And I think people don't want to invest that time or don't feel they have the time – they have other priorities. Now in the military, it's quite clear that you don't have that luxury. You have to develop your teams. And ultimately, when you go on operations, that pays dividends.

The risk depends on the culture of your organization. Does it reward results, or does it reward decisions? In the military, you reward people for being decisive, as long as those decisions have been made rationally, with logic behind them, because in that environment doing something is better than doing nothing. If you only reward based on results, you inadvertently create a culture of risk-averseness.

JEREMY: If I put a leader in front of you, what would you tell them are the key benefits that come out of the hard work to get this in place?

JAMES: Well, first of all, they will get discretionary effort from people. Because fundamentally, whatever endeavor we take part in as humans, we want to be valued as part of a team and feel that someone's investing in us.

If you are communicating efficiently at all levels, up and down and horizontally, you will be able to seize the opportunities that will always appear at the edges of any organization. You've created this really energetic, agile organization that is working toward one unified purpose, which is ultimately efficient.

In the military, you're always trained to work on the 30–70 rule: that you shouldn't make a decision with less than 30% of the information. However, 30% is good enough to make a viable call, and an informed guess; 70% is about as good as you're ever going to get. If you wait for more, you're going to be overwhelmed by events and will ultimately fail, and more agile players will take advantage of that. In my view, the people who have been the most successful leaders, and who have created the greatest culture, are the people who see risk as an opportunity, and not as something to try and avoid.

JEREMY: We talk about a 70% solution being OK, but you're talking about a 30% solution being OK – now that's agile. But we do get things wrong, so what is the negative side of empowering others? What can happen if people fail?

JAMES: Well, this all comes down to accountability. Often, people misunderstand mission command, as: "I've given clear direction, why did that person not do something?" In my mind, that means there's been a breakdown in communication somewhere along the line. You have to constantly ensure that communication is clear. However, equally, you've got to have the moral courage to call out bad behaviors. Because there's no point talking about this if one person's not buying into it. Even if they've been empowered, they can be toxic in the organization, and so you just have to be watchful in calling that out. That can be challenging if that person is your top performer or has a lot of credibility.

But also, you have to make sure the communication is clear because the worst-case scenario is that people start behaving in a consent-and-evade method. I've seen that in the military: people agree that there's a clear direction, but they've got to a point where they're so empowered that they're overconfident in their abilities as they start to make their own decisions. They may be doing this for well-intentioned reasons, but, ultimately, they might not see the bigger picture and there can be huge unintended consequences from doing that.

So you just have to be vigilant in watching for bad behaviors when they start creeping in, and also people taking shortcuts, and you've got to stamp down on it.

JEREMY: A follow-up question on that point: if you have people who don't play ball, who fail fast but don't learn from it – what happens if those individuals are at the very top of the organization? What do you do about that?

JAMES: That is the ultimate challenge. If you have a toxic culture at the top, then this approach is never going to work, because you will not have psychological safety. That toxicity is going to filter all the way down. That, in my view, is something that boards should look very closely at: have you got the right people in senior positions, and are they showing the right behaviors?

JEREMY: Any parting words?

JAMES: The key mantra I've always adopted, which was told to me early on at the academies, was: never tell people how to do things; tell people what to do and they'll surprise you with their ingenuity. In essence, this is about how you get ordinary people to do extraordinary things, which can sometimes be against their best interests personally, but aligned to organizational and team goals.

SIX

Measuring Employee Empowerment

In this final chapter, we'll learn about:

- The 90-Day Road Map Tracker for in-role CEOs and their line managers to measure progress week-by-week

- The Six Centers of Me model for assessing progress at a personal and emotional level

- Cultural measures of success at the organization level

When organizations are making a fundamental shift to encourage their brightest and best to unleash their inner CEOs, there of course needs to be a return on that effort and investment.

To quote the adage: "What gets measured gets done." When we're measuring the newly unleashed in-role CEOs, we should use a combination of two sets of measurables, at the personal and the organizational level. When these come together, it is possible to assess the effects of individuals and their teams stepping up and taking ownership, and the impact it has on the business.

As we've covered, this is exciting and productive because it creates a positive ripple effect, extending far beyond job role results alone. It's also worth noting that while we must measure our unleashed inner CEOs, we must continue to measure how boards, executive leaders and line managers are stepping up and if the culture of the organization is adapting to create an environment where unleashed inner CEOs at all levels thrive.

This chapter provides detailed guidance for measuring progress at the individual level. It then provides a series of questions relevant to gathering both qualitative and quantitative data at the organizational level, with a focus on employee engagement and the impact of this on external branding, as well as on turnover and internal employee satisfaction measures.

Tracking the progress of in-role CEOs is essential. The organization and the individual are collectively responsible for taking ownership of the measurements of empowerment when unleashing inner CEOs. It is not down to the individual alone nor to line managers. The nature of stepping up means operating as a leader, taking responsibility for themselves, for their team and their results. Milvio DiBartolemeo gives a wonderful example of this in action:

> "As an empowered contributor, I lead by example. For example, instead of raising problems to line or senior management, I offered options, being conscious that you are either solving problems for people or causing problems for people."

Enabling a culture of empowerment such as this requires root-and-branch involvement.

90-Day Road Map Tracker

It's critical to measure results from day one, so to help with that, I've devised a checklist to track the completion of the 90-Day Road Map activities as detailed in Chapter 4. The 90-Day Road Map Tracker is aimed at individuals who are using the road map to unleash their inner CEO. You'll see the same twelve weeks of activities as in the road map table, but this time it's about measuring the progress and impact. This final table completes the toolkit and is simple to follow. I'll take you through an outline of the tracker.

Week 1

As you can see, Week 1 is about setting and agreeing on the parameters within which to operate. In the Measure column, you would aim to have a signed-off road map and plan, as well as senior-level alignment. The agreed training, coaching and mentor resources would be in place, and the key people at senior level would be fully briefed. The 4Es assessment would be completed as part of your first week's activities.

Week 2

For Week 2 measurements, the first training course or session would be completed or underway. Candidates would be familiar with the 4Es and will have generated new projects or ideas they will be working on during their 90-Day Road Map.

Week 3

In Week 3, the project team would have been activated, and feedback gathered on the plan, which will be refined if necessary. There will have been a one-to-one with the manager mentor to go through the assessment results and to subsequently create a personal development plan, including relevant self-help resources.

Week 4

By the end of Week 4, the project would be in progress and you would have a collaborative communication framework supported by some kind of digital tool to manage the project, which would be set up for, shared with, explained to and understood by all members of the team. You will have evidence of progress via formal project tracking and updates, enabled by a mobile-first tool like Trello or an internal platform. A project management course would have been organized by now if needed.

Figure 17: *90-Day Road Map Tracker*

Week 5

With your first month's review completed, both job performance and unleashed inner CEO performance will have been tracked. You will have the opportunity to talk about what has been achieved, the roadblocks you have faced, and your expected performance for the next month, based on what's happened in the first month. Your plan for the next 30 days will be refined a little bit further with personal development, prioritization and expectations.

Week 6

By Week 6, formalized co-working sessions for self-development should have been completed, as well as a one-to-one with the manager and mentor to debrief and feed into the ongoing development plan, which may be further tweaked after the review of actions. There will also have been a review of what has been executed through your project tracking and a chance to go in a slightly different direction, refine your approach or choose to continue in the same way.

Week 7

This is about evidenced ownership of self-development through a completed learning log, which will be based on the Personal Development Mosaic actions and formalized company training that has been attended. This is the first opportunity, after seven weeks, to review what you have learned and what is needed to move forward. The other measurement will be a review of project activities and milestones on the current plan.

Questions to ask at this stage would be:

- Are you delivering as per expectations?
- Do you have any roadblocks?
- Is there a plan B in place?
- Do you need to discuss the plan further with a line manager to create a road map of corrective action?
- Is there interim communication with the project team as you approach another completed month?
- Is there clarity of direction, and are there progress issues, solutions and actions going forward, along with any amendments you're making to the project, the timeline or the team?

Week 8

By the end of this week, a full review should have been completed and the plan for the next thirty days agreed. Tracking of both job and unleashed inner CEO performance is required.

Questions to ask at this stage would be:

- Are you still achieving what you need to within your job role, as you follow the plan to unleash your inner CEO?
- How is your project progressing in terms of deliverables, collaboration with others and communication clarity, both vertically and horizontally?
- Have you got clarity on what you need to achieve in the next thirty days?

This is an excellent opportunity, after eight weeks, for an informal feedback loop around knowledge, skills, behaviors, progress, unleashed strengths and gaps from not only your line manager but also your project team.

Week 9

The measurement here is about answering the key questions and evaluating the actions you implemented following the Week 8 review. Personal development, progress updates, mutual feedback to note what's going well and what pressure points are emerging, provide an overall temperature check. The temperature check can also relate to the qualitative emotional factor, covered previously, in addition to tangible goals achieved.

Imperative across Weeks 9 and 10 is a focus on project deliverables and ensuring you are on top of your specific job role must-dos.

Week 10

This is about continuing management of the project and team, which may require another one-to-one session to review results, progress and objectives. This could be supplemented through informal feedback discussions with members of the project team and other stakeholders to gather further directional advice and personal development tweaks. Week 10 is similar to the previous week, so the primary measure of success is the same.

Week 11

This week requires a formal project review with the manager and mentor, a look at the results so far, a consideration of informal and formal feedback from others and, finally, the planning for the presentation to the CEO in the final week. This can include role-playing, one-to-one coaching support and other forms of practice to ensure a high degree of personal readiness.

Week 12

The final week will be measured by the delivery of the presentation to the CEO or other senior-level person, and the consideration of actual qualitative and quantitative results set in Week 1 and refined throughout the 90-Day Road Map where relevant. Formal feedback from seniors, peers and the project team will then be discussed with your manager and mentor. The plan for the next 90 days will be agreed, with supporting learning and development in place.

The goal for the end of the twelve weeks is to have achieved an ongoing, measured discussion throughout the process. The business will know the qualitative and quantitative impacts of what's happening at an organizational and personal level. There should be no surprises for anyone involved because open discussions, adjustments and tracking have been constant since Week 1.

This completes the current cycle of the 90-Day Road Map and is a perfect time for a period of reflection, not just for those who have been unleashing their inner CEO, but for all leaders and managers involved. Completion of the 90-Day Road Map is a big commitment as well as a significant measurement in itself, so it's an opportunity to take a breath and review what's been achieved at the personal and organizational levels. Finally, I recommend that an agreement for the next 4Es progress assessments should be completed, which ought to happen in the range of six to nine months following the initial assessment.

The Six Centers of Me

Now it's time to make things personal. There's an emotional and personal side to the qualitative element of unleashing the inner CEO. The Six Centers of Me is a helpful model for assessing progress with this. It can be translated into quantitative impact by asking individuals to give ratings as part of the discussion, for example on a five-point Likert scale from "Strongly agree" to "Strongly disagree". It's about getting a real sense of immersion in this new way of operating; about understanding how it impacts the individual and, in turn, the impact on others, the business and the working environment.

The model is made up of six topics for reflection. The questions themselves can be owned and considered by each in-role CEO, and then form part of a coaching conversation with their line manager or other stakeholders.

The Six Centers of Me provides a temperature check from an emotional standpoint, which we don't often talk about, certainly not often enough. We know we're heading in the right direction because there are things we can do at the quantitative level that relate very clearly to the organizational activities and actions in the 90-Day Road Map. Both the quantitative component and the qualitative elements (such as the Six Centers of Me) are critical for success.

Furthermore, the Six Centers of Me is a tangible model for people to take ownership of and measure their experience, which is a complex thing to do. This is the all-important emotional side to personal development, of which we must be aware. For this to really come alive, involving the line manager, HR and other stakeholders in the conversation will help to establish the facts as well as the feelings, identifying progress while looking toward supported, personal development action.

My Center of Autonomy

My first center is autonomy. Do I feel a degree of independence, empowerment and freedom from constraints to unleash my inner CEO in my job role and beyond?

My Center of Self-Motivation

My second center is self-motivation. Am I energized and able to achieve my personal vision with commitment and enthusiasm, without feeling pressure from others?

My Center of Self-Confidence

My third center is my belief that I have the capability, energy and skills for success as an unleashed CEO.

My Center of Self-Efficacy

My fourth center is self-efficacy. Do I have the ability to control and deliver desired results for me, the team and the organization?

My Center of Job Satisfaction

My fifth center is job satisfaction. Do I feel appropriately recognized and rewarded for my contribution above and beyond my specific job role?

My Center of Relationships

My sixth center is about relationships. Are my relationships meaningful, collaborative and productive? Am I able to bring others along with me at all levels as I contribute beyond my specific job role?

Figure 18: *The Six Centers of Me*

Cultural measures of success at the organization level

A culture of compliance encourages bureaucracy in organizations and is characterized by habits such as risk-averse decision-making among management. Conversely, a culture of autonomy focuses on how to best service customers and employees. Managers coach their teams, rather than merely assigning them tasks. As a result, employee engagement is higher and staff turnover is lower. Decision-making should be occurring at every level of the organization, which is precisely what we're aiming for in unleashing inner CEOs. Rasie Bamigbade describes the impact of empowerment on the wider organization:

"There was a significant increase in morale, an increase in employee referrals and an increase in the bottom line."

In her article, "Empower employees to make things happen",[33] Marina Krakovsky examines how organizations have traditionally operated in a culture of compliance but need to transition to a culture of autonomy for a more productive workplace. She offers the example of a manufacturing company with around 11,000 employees who didn't feel able to voice concerns under a top-down decision-making and management approach:

"After a new CEO set more customer-centric goals for the company, empowerment began spreading as a natural consequence, she says. Once employees knew what the goal of 'delighting customers' looked like, they began to speak up when an order wasn't meeting specs."

This is at the heart of the shift I'm proposing that organizations make to create in-role CEOs. It's natural for us to want to be part of something bigger than ourselves. If everybody has permission to speak up, we can find ways to do things more efficiently and customer satisfaction will increase. In turn, when employees feel appreciated and that they're doing something worthwhile, their satisfaction increases too. When we're looking at an empowered organization – which is what unleashing inner CEOs at every level creates – there's going to be a significant impact on the company culture. This would show up in everyday work as individuals demonstrating a can-do attitude.

Below is a list of questions. Board members, the C-suite, HR and L&D leads should ask themselves these questions to identify behavior change across the organization. In addition, and just as importantly, insights can be gathered from individual contributors across the organization by asking the same questions (for example, in the form of a pulse survey). Doing this can itself be motivating and awareness-raising for your teams, as well as generating insightful data. The questions are:

- What evidence is there that the 90-Day Road Map is driving a positive mindset within the company as a whole?

- How are the developments impacting organizational culture and levels of employee engagement?

- To what extent is increased collaboration and communication happening?

- Where across the organization am I able to notice emerging leadership management traits?

- What attitudinal changes are evident; for example, do employees seem content when you interact with them? Do they seem more resilient in the face of challenges?

- Are we building the culture of autonomy we promised, rather than just talking about it?

When taking on new projects and operating with greater autonomy, it will be necessary for in-role CEOs to handle situations and pressures that they may not have had to deal with in the old hierarchy. As we covered in the toolkit, a solution-oriented culture here is paramount.

In terms of the organization's duty of care, as you empower people to unleash their inner CEO, I like this quote from Ian Hutchinson, author of *People Glue*: "Your number one customers are your people. Look after employees first and then customers last."[34] I like this perspective because it keeps in mind that there are people in the organization whom we need to accompany on their journey. After all, they're going to need support. When we support and recognize them, we have the opportunity to help them excel in the long term, not just generate short-term gains. In summary, the qualitative element measures are what we're looking for in a person's development. They become the driver of high performance, strong contribution and growth.

Once we have recognized the importance of managing cultural and individual measures, we can also consider the quantifiable efforts to prove the impact on core internal measures and external business growth.

A few considerations might be:

- To what extent is employee satisfaction increasing?

- What evidence of impact are we starting to see through our customers, partners and other stakeholders externally?

- What specific benefits are our customers experiencing?

- How are customer satisfaction measures being impacted? Are customers noticing a difference?

- Is our business growing?

- Can we separate our organic growth curve and incremental revenue gains by unleashing our inner CEOs?

- What is the impact on our overall bottom line and functional KPIs?

- How are the developments put in place to unleash inner CEOs impacting attraction, recruitment and retention of our workforce?

- How are our employer branding measures being impacted?

It will be important to embed ways of asking these questions throughout the organization; for example, as part of regular consultations with everyone, at all levels. This way, examples of success as well as patches of slower implementation can be identified and explored.

Putting people first

"To win in the marketplace, you must first win in the workplace."[35] This is a great quote from Doug Conant, ex-CEO of Campbell Soup Company. To realize the results we are targeting, we've got to focus internally on creating the foundation and climate for in-role CEOs to thrive. This requires work, at all levels, on mindset, culture, workplace practices and workforce effectiveness, because these are the things that will impact the quantitative measurements at the organizational level.

This includes, for example, internal engagement measures, employee satisfaction improvement and the organization's overall employer branding performance, internally as much as externally. Not only will this contribute to business growth, but it will also help assess how much more attractive the organization is to those seeking employment. Particularly those who want to be part of something exciting and empowering, whether they are looking for a permanent position, or are a part of the growing independent workforce engaged by companies globally.

This is a relatively new battleground from a marketing, recruitment and retention perspective. Organizations must find ways to measure whether employees feel more connected to the company and explore how to increase connection. Potential employers must become more appealing as people appraise them and decide whether they'd like to work for them. Get this right, and it pays dividends, as Milvio DiBartolemeo describes:

> "I was able to attract and recruit the very best people particularly for highly specialized portfolio, program and project roles where the market is quite constrained. With my team and the broader business area where leaders are empowered and can positively influence change, turnover is non-existent. People are happy, work together well and have a willingness to continuously improve."

To attract loyal employees and top talent, be it a permanent or independent resource, organizations need to ensure that potential recruits reviewing their employment options can see certain things clearly. For example:

- Does the company have a great way of working?
- Does it have a great structure in place?
- How high is employee turnover? Is it reducing?

It's worth bearing in mind that potential employees can often see online reviews, so it's essential to manage the company's reputation, not only among customers but across the board both internally and externally. Tim Lupinacci says,

> "Part of it does tie back to the idea of being able to recruit and retain motivated talent. They have a seat at the table, they're engaged, it trickles through the company. The collective impact on culture, and its underpinning values and behaviors, is tangible. That level of buy-in and belief leads to a better organization and I can say, hand on heart, that it leads to better financial results."

What next?

In the final chapter, we'll look at the bigger picture of what I've shared throughout this book and the incredible opportunity we now have to reimagine our organizations amid continuing global uncertainty, disruption and an increasingly distributed workforce.

First, our final interviewee, global learning leader and specialist, Philippe Bonnet, considers what happens when organizations unlock the power of their people and unleash distributed leadership. Philippe passionately believes in the power of collective and collaborative leadership and how it can multiply business growth efforts.

Interview with Philippe Bonnet

Philippe Bonnet is a former vice-president, global head of learning and organizational development and HR business partner at Essilor International and is now a C-suite executive coach. He combines senior management experience in diverse, multicultural business environments with longstanding expertise in coaching at the executive level. His passion lies with people and equipping teams with the knowledge, skills and behaviors needed to thrive and grow in an increasingly uncertain workplace.

JEREMY: In the spirit of unleashing the Inner CEO within our people, what must be in place at the organizational level for this to take off and succeed?

PHILIPPE: To get people to buy into the vision, you need to be able to sell it to them. As a company, if you talk about what you aim to become, and bring people along on that journey by mobilizing them behind your purpose, you create the climate for engagement, commitment and success, which is perfect for unleashing inner CEOs.

JEREMY: What skillsets do our unleashed inner CEOs need to display to ultimately be successful in and beyond their job role?

PHILIPPE: They have to be able to deliver results, and have a command of broader business capabilities beyond their job role. Communication and the ability to influence and inspire, no matter what level they are at in the company, are at the heart of it. You have to help people grow those skills quickly as they start their leadership journey at their level, getting behind them with the right training, mentoring and coaching support.

JEREMY: Why do you think it is so vital for organizations to embrace a flatter structure and truly empower people to unleash their inner CEO?

PHILIPPE: Simply put, it's because of the speed of the transformation we are experiencing. We need to adapt and do things differently. A traditional leader cannot adapt quickly and must mobilize the power of curated leadership. Leaders at all levels need to deliver results in their jobs and contribute to the health of the whole business, whether at the strategic or operational level. This has to happen fast because speed changes a lot of things, such as how we think about our businesses, how we structure them and how we must continually adapt.

Embracing that simple shift and including everyone in the journey is the first step to creating an environment and culture where curated leadership can flourish. That has to be driven by those at the top, and trust in those executive leaders is critical for people to buy into the vision. However, that trust is easy to lose if they aren't authentic, and their behavior and modeling can be the difference between success or failure.

JEREMY: It can positively affect how our unleashed CEOs model themselves when they look up the line and observe the behaviors and actions of their executive leaders, so it's important that they have the right motivations. Do you agree?

PHILIPPE: We need to ensure that our people have the right motivations to step up and deliver more, supported by the company but also within their evolving leadership brand. That is how I see curated leadership.

Many people are leading at all levels, in different ways, and it's those differences that have the most impact. We need different leadership styles and skillsets for various projects, situations and challenges. It's crucial that, at the organizational level, we support this development with targeted, personalized learning as well as standard approaches. We need mentoring and coaching to support the process and to bring out the best leadership traits in our unleashed inner CEOs. This is empowerment that works; without the necessary support, it will evaporate and fail, creating a negative legacy.

JEREMY: From your perspective as a global learning leader, how should organizations support their people as they unleash their inner CEOs?

PHILIPPE: To support this goal, I recommend that companies appoint a new kind of CEO: a chief empowerment officer. If our executive leaders, including the current CEO, repurpose their role with this mindset, it builds a successful path to follow.

JEREMY: Like me, you have lived and worked on a global scale for many years; how does the concept of empowering others and unleashing the inner CEOs in our companies operate across borders and cultures?

PHILIPPE: People's national and social cultures, as well as company cultures, are significant influences. For example, an international company working in Japan or Brazil that embraces the "think global – work local" approach and tailors it to provide the best for its employees, can get the best out of the international situation. You can create the environment where you empower people to a higher degree than a local company typically would, so it's seen as an advantage rather than a disadvantage. This personalized approach removes bias, encourages inclusion and creates a greater sense of belonging, where varied ways of operating are embraced and developed for the benefit of everyone.

For this to be effective, you have to be able to track results from a business and a personal perspective, so I recommend also appointing a chief evaluation officer and a chief emotion officer to structure and personalize the approach on a deeper level.

JEREMY: What's the impact on the organization, internally and externally, when we successfully unleash inner CEOs?

PHILIPPE: The critical impact to measure is the extra value or the additional engagement we derive from our people. It revolves around the intangibles – engagement, motivation, commitment and collaborative mindset – which is essential because if you don't measure these, the day will come when your people stop putting in the extra effort and focus purely on their job role. Think of impact as an iceberg; what you see are the tangible features, but what supports it is underneath. You could argue that qualitative intangibles are more relevant to measure from day one than anything else. Do it well – support and encourage the process, and the measurables will look after themselves.

Take the PSA Group (the Peugeot group of companies), for example. Its profitability, customer satisfaction measures and quality consistency were high, and the leader at the time [2020] recognized that this was driven as much by individual commitment and passion as by hitting tangible targets, and announced that for those who contributed to the results, he was going to give €4,100 to every employee who earned less than double the minimum salary. This was the part of the workforce that didn't usually receive a bonus like the rest of the organization. A part, nonetheless, who were central to success, and who had unleashed their inner CEOs – and they were rightly rewarded for it.

JEREMY: Considering the overall theme of unleashing the inner CEOs within our people: if organizations don't do it, what's the cost of maintaining the status quo?

PHILIPPE: It's the loss of opportunity, lack of innovation and an inability to attract and retain the talent the company needs. It may still survive for a time, but only through short-term focus and fighting on the frontlines, which is not sustainable for long-term business health. The companies that embrace a mentality of experimentation and acknowledge the power within their people, will have the greatest success.

Conclusion

We have a huge opportunity to ambitiously reimagine our organizations around the empowering, collective and collaborative framework of distributed leadership. There has never been a better time to unleash inner CEOs across all levels and involve them in redesigning businesses to make distributed leadership a reality. The evidence that organizations can adapt and change quickly is undeniable – see, for example, the normalization of more flexible work models that are now trumping the office-based approaches favored before the pandemic of the early 2020s. Many companies with legacy structures and ways of working used the opportunity to break from the past and create a new future for the way the company and its people operated, with greater autonomy and with the customer at the heart of decision-making at all levels.

This more flexible way of working is now dominant in the West, with the likes of Ocado, Spotify, Disney, Nationwide, NatWest, Unilever, Morgan Stanley and more leading the way.[36] As we look east to Asia Pacific, we see a similar picture, with over 85% of companies in the region optimizing hybrid work arrangements, according to a survey by telecommunications firm Telstra.[37] This new reality is proof that radical change *can* happen – and quickly.

One such company linking flexible working structures and processes with a new sense of bold empowerment is the global consulting firm, Protiviti. This is an organization that believes hybrid working is the perfect situation for distributed leadership. First, they empower employees to make decisions about how they work and from where they work. Second, they build the values and behaviors (at a cultural level) to ensure that all-level decision-making has client needs, and the company's purpose, at heart. In an interview with Katie Kuener-Hebert, Protiviti's EVP of global human resources, Scott Redfearn, explains how the company has used the change in working models to fast-track a more empowering culture internally, to better service clients externally:

"Empowerment is a key component of our culture at Protiviti and at the core of our hybrid work strategy. Our people are empowered to make decisions about where and how they work to serve clients, develop additional skills for greater impact and achieve the flexibility that teams need. By focusing on the purpose of what we are doing and the value we are creating, our people are seeing their work in terms of purpose and impact, rather than location. We have seen our people trusting each other to do what's right for the firm, our clients and our teams – across all levels."[38]

Collective and collaborative leadership

Protiviti has fast-tracked the flatter organizational structures I have been talking about throughout the book and has provided a new framework for managing a highly engaged workforce, one which is more empowered, collaborative, supportive and aligned. This point is further reinforced in Petra Kuenkel's book, *The Art of Leading Collectively: Co-creating a sustainable, socially just future,*[39] which I highly recommend.

A more collective approach to leadership is the secret to sustained, shared success and mutual growth. I have built on this to propose that "collective and collaborative leadership" glue two elements together: collective leadership and the mindset of collaborating to grow. Like many things I have proposed in this book, it starts with mindset and then shifts into implementing and operating to become "the way we do things around here".

Figure 19: *Collective and Collaborative Leadership model*

The concepts, ideas and actions proposed in this book are designed to help organizations build their own version of collective and collaborative leadership by unleashing the inner CEOs across their organizations. In implementing them, you will discover best practices, traps to avoid and watch-outs to keep in mind. You will be able to fast-track your own next practices, as you encourage your organization to unleash its inner CEOs. Empowerment, ownership of ideas, creativity and innovation come from our distributed leaders, allowing us to build a more resilient business model from the ground up.

We have experienced a pandemic, and now, as we move into new ways of working and doing business, with largely hybrid models, we're operating in a VUCAD world: volatile, uncertain, complex, ambiguous and distributed. This isn't just an experiment; it's the new normal.

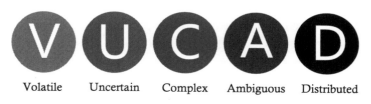

Volatile   Uncertain   Complex   Ambiguous   Distributed

Figure 20: *VUCAD*

By building a new, more resilient business model now, we'll create a structure that can more easily adapt for the VUCAD future. Organizations will be better able to shift and evolve, rather than be forced into broader and deeper transformation.

In the interviews throughout this book, our experts have reinforced and demonstrated the in-role CEO model in a multitude of different roles, industries, backgrounds and cultures. They all have one thing in common: they support and encourage unleashing the inner CEOs within our organizations to make leadership at all levels a reality. They see this as the next important and urgent step in corporate evolution and have been championing the cause in their own ways. The interviews are designed to serve as a barometer to measure progress: they are a temperature check for companies to assess their roadblocks, their opportunities, their starting points and the milestones on their journey to enabling successful distributed leadership. The interviewees have done this and are still doing it. Their commentary supports the ideas in this book and provides a glimpse of what could happen when you do it.

Many of the interviewee experts observed that horizontal power is vital and that the vertical, hierarchical way of doing things is no longer helpful (while acknowledging that there still needs to be some form of hierarchy in place to lead and manage the new era). They reinforced the need for flatter structures so that leaders can navigate the choppy waters of the future, help unleash inner CEOs and execute and protect short- and medium-term goals. Perhaps it's not quite the full holacracy I mentioned earlier, but it's certainly a more collective and collaborative approach to the leadership of our organizations.

Tim Lupinacci describes how important this shift is for developing a more entrepreneurial approach:

"We're rethinking models and how people work. The shift we are seeing now is from [legal] partnerships to business leadership. Building a culture of bold empowerment is a game-changer in this respect. People can go beyond the strict structures of the past and embrace a more multi-faceted, interesting and empowering role."

The other commonality that stands out from the interviews is that organizations can embrace a diversity of skillsets, trumping the old style of power or skills held onto by the few. In the recent past, it was common to have special projects, populated with a chosen few. The same kind of environment would reserve expert training, coaching and "talent tracks" for selected individuals. By definition, this was exclusive.

If we are to unleash our inner CEOs, we must think more inclusively. With more diverse skillsets developing in more people, there's a better opportunity to reinvent the business within the more resilient, future-geared framework we've discussed. It's an exciting time because when we have more leaders at all levels in the organization, who are knowledgeable, skilled and modeling the desired behaviors, it means we can truly unleash the power of our people, supported by modern structures, processes, training and coaching. This challenges human capital and HR leaders to step up and support this bold, human transformation to create unleashed, empowered, motivated and valued in-role CEOs across our population of permanent employees and valued independent and contractor resources.

Unleashing in-role CEOs helps executive leaders focus on the strategic bigger picture and build new ecosystems whereby people can more easily contribute; in which solutions are more tailored; where networks are more collective; and for which everyone takes ownership and is accountable.

To conclude, I'll summarize the key messages that have emerged as critical factors for success in a new manifesto for successful distributed leadership.

1   A new and empowering leadership mindset at board and executive leadership level.

2   An evolved culture underpinned by behaviors and values that are consistent with the desire to unleash leadership at all levels and empower people to new heights.

3   Clear vision, expectations and direction from executive leaders, communicated to all.

4   A shift in mindset throughout the organization to underpin willing, safe action as in-role CEOs.

5   A platform of psychological safety reinforced by human capital and human resource leaders to enable everyone to have the courage to step up, to make mistakes without being judged, to be supported and to feel safe to challenge the status quo with open debate and feedback.

6   A climate that supports experimentation, learning from failure and rapid adoption of next practices. This should be supported and fully enabled by appropriate digital technologies and tools for the benefit of the workforce internally, unlocking more effective customer focus externally.

7   A reimagined, flatter organizational structure that removes layers of hierarchy and encourages horizontal management principles that support performance and the development of leaders at all levels.

8   Repurposed line management support underpinned by a growth mindset, driving a strong coaching-led approach with in-role CEOs. This represents the shift from performance management to performance support.

9   A road map of actions measured from day one, including assessment, action review, behavior recognition and ongoing results.

10   A bold learning and development support plan to provide the strategic and operational knowledge, skills and behaviors required for leaders at all levels.

11   Evolved recognition and reward indicators that catch people doing it right, beyond the numbers.

12   Embedding the changes culturally, to represent the evolved values and behaviors that fuel the reality of distributed leadership.

Figure 21: *The blueprint for successful distributed leadership*

Ultimately, all of this will allow in-role CEOs to grow as high-contributing leaders at all levels. This in turn supports their own macro leadership journey as they contribute more broadly, rise through the business and develop their own career path.

Everyone needs to be accountable and responsible for growth, both theirs and that of the organization. Engaged, mobilized and motivated people are central to creating this ideal environment, which links to satisfaction in a job role, attracts talent into the business and helps to retain great people. Attraction and retention take care of themselves in this context, whether that's with a permanent workforce or an increasingly loyal independent workforce of people who want to work for you and with you.

Further support, training and guidance

I have a series of supportive keynote talks, consulting, training and coaching solutions, available globally, for organizations that are ready to accept the challenge of becoming a twenty-first-century business, unleashing their inner CEOs and embracing a new collective and collaborative approach to the power of distributed leadership of their business. These include:

- Keynote sessions to introduce the concept to your wider audience

- Leadership briefings for boards, executive and NEDs and leaders

- Organizational briefing sessions tailored to your specific needs, challenges and opportunities

- Working with HR to provide a more suitable human capital framework to support the implementation

- Training sessions for managers and your distributed leader network

- Developmental support for those in-role CEOs stepping out beyond their day-to-day job and demonstrating leadership at their level

All my consulting, briefings, coaching and training materials are designed to unleash the inner CEOs within our organizations and to help grow their knowledge, skills and behaviors for ultimate business success. They can be delivered virtually or face to face, supported by a global network of experts.

I am ready to support *you*.

AN EXCLUSIVE OFFER FROM JEREMY TO ALL READERS

Claim your digital artwork proof and access special discounts off my services and support

To celebrate the launch of *Unleash the Inner CEO – Make distributed leadership a reality*, I have partnered with BlockRank to give each reader an opportunity to claim their unique digital artwork proof. There are free versions that everyone can claim, and rarer digital artworks, with associated services for organizations to bid for, which will give you immediate access to my consulting support in your transformation efforts.

To claim your free *Unleash the Inner CEO* digital artwork proof, simply click on the QR code here:

Your digital proof will be your guarantee of authenticity and will provide each person with a 5% discount off any of my services and solutions (ie speaking engagements, trainings, consulting, coaching, and more), which you can see here: www. performanceworks.global

Access the rare and for sale *Unleash the Inner CEO* digital artworks here

Organizations, businesses and public institutions can bid for or purchase one of the exclusive rare digital proofs, which will come with generous discounts of up to 50% when purchasing any of my support services.

In addition, a few of the rarer digital artworks will also grant access to a suite of free keynotes, free copies of my book, free leadership briefings, and free consulting, to help you make distributed leadership a reality in your organization.

Your digital artwork proof is redeemable now from my partner, BlockRank, through this exclusive QR code, as the next step in your distributed leadership and organizational transformation journey. You will be required to sign up for their secure digital wallet to house your artwork in the Blockchain, protecting it securely, forever.

For those purchasing the rare digital artworks, you will get a direct message from me to start our conversation and collaboration.

Partnering with BlockRank

In providing these digital artworks, I am a proud partner of BlockRank, powered by HQNFTs, a leading edge blockchain and artificial intelligence (AI) solutions company that connects the dots between people and technology.

BlockRank develops and implements real world, practical, and scalable solutions for government and enterprise organizations as they accelerate their digital transformational journey from Web2 to Web3.

Eighty-eight percent of Fortune 500 companies operating in the 1950s no longer exist today. Lack of innovation was stated as the main cause. This is an even bigger risk for 21st century companies slow to transform. BlockRank's aim is to help accelerate progress through enabling first-mover advantage for organizations wishing to bullet-proof their future by being the prime disruptor in their industry and the first entering this new Web3 frontier in a meaningful, measurable way.

BlockRank's impressive use cases include transport, smart cities, security, supply chain, and finance.

> "BlockRank's technology could give us up to a ten-year advantage on our competitors."
> (CEO, Global security company)

Message BlockRank here to find out how they can help your organization: success@hqnfts.xyz

Notes

1 CF Bolster, *An Exploration of the Relationship Between Acts of Courage and the Development of Personal Empowerment* (Case Western Reserve University ProQuest Dissertations Publishing, 1996)

2 C Chavez and S Palsule, *Rehumanizing Leadership: Putting purpose back into business* (LID, 2020)

3 J McLung and G Vaynerchuk, 'Innovate or Die' (2017), www.youtube.com/watch?v=WdYtoj4KSeU, accessed 4 November 2023

4 I Bezek, '7 companies that went bankrupt due to Covid', *US News* (12 May 2023), https://money.usnews.com/investing/stock-market-

news/slideshows/covid-bankrupt-companies, accessed 9 November 2023

5   B Heater, N Mascarenhas and A Ha, 'Remembering the startups we lost in 2020', *Tech Crunch* (22 December 2020), https://techcrunch.com/2020/12/22/remember-the-startups-we-lost-in-2020, accessed 4 November 2023

6   For more information, see Ethereum, *Introduction to Web 3* (12 April 2023), https://ethereum.org/en/web3, accessed 4 November 2023

7   L Appleton, 'A growing threat: Protecting your business from cyber crime in 2023' (Elitegroup. com, 19 April 2023), www.elitegroup.com/resources/blogs/cybercrime-trends-2023, accessed 4 November 2023

8   Bridges and Performance Works, *Transforming Your Company into a Digital-Driven Business* (Bridges Business Consultancy Int & PerformanceWorks International, 2019), www.bridgesconsultancy.com/wp-content/uploads/2016/10/Transforming-Your-Company-into-a-Digital-Driven-Business.pdf, accessed 20 December 2023

9   J Blain and R Haynes, 'The blended workforce revolution' (Performance Works, 2020), https://performanceworks.global/wp-content/uploads/2020/10/The-Blended-Workforce-Revolution-Whitepaper.pdf, accessed 4 November 2023

10 J Winsor, 'New book from Harvard Business
    Review Press' (John Winsor, 2023), https://
    johnwinsor.com/open-talent-book, accessed
    4 November 2023

11 OECD, *Skills for the Digital Transition: Assessing
    recent trends using big data* (2022), www.oecd.org/
    employment/skills-for-the-digital-transition-
    38c36777-en.htm, accessed 4 November 2022

12 R Speculand, *World's Best Bank: A strategic
    guide to digital transformation* (Bridges Business
    Consultancy Int, 2021)

13 Your FLOCK, 'Is hybrid working for your
    business?' (nd), https://yourflock.co.uk,
    accessed 4 November 2023

14 Bridges and Performance Works, *Transforming
    Your Company into a Digital-Driven Business*
    (Bridges Business Consultancy Int &
    PerformanceWorks International, 2019),
    www.bridgesconsultancy.com/wp-content/
    uploads/2016/10/Transforming-Your-
    Company-into-a-Digital-Driven-Business.pdf,
    accessed 20 December 2023

15 McKinsey, 'Building a tech-enabled ecosystem:
    An interview with Ping An's Jessica Tan'
    (McKinsey Quarterly, December 2018),
    www.mckinsey.com/~/media/McKinsey/
    Featured%20Insights/China/Building%20
    a%20tech%20enabled%20ecosystem%20
    An%20interview%20with%20Ping%20Ans%20
    Jessica%20Tan/Building-a-tech-enabled-

ecosystem-An-interview-with-Ping-Ans-Jessica-Tan.pdf, accessed 4 November 2023

16   M Diaz, 'ChatGPT vs. Bing Chat vs. Google Bard: Which is the best AI chatbot?' (ZEDNET, 29 September 2023), www.zdnet.com/article/chatgpt-vs-bing-chat-vs-google-bard-which-is-the-best-ai-chatbot, accessed 9 November 2023

17   M Coulter and G Bensinger, 'Alphabet shares dive after Google AI chatbot Bard flubs answer in ad', *Reuters* (9 February 2023), www.reuters.com/technology/google-ai-chatbot-bard-offers-inaccurate-information-company-ad-2023-02-08, accessed 9 November 2023

18   V Jouany, 'Empowerment in the workplace: Definition and best practices' (Haiilo Blog, 19 January 2023), https://haiilo.com/blog/empowerment-in-the-workplace-enable-your-employees, accessed 5 November 2023

19   AC Edmondson, 'Psychological safety' (nd), https://amycedmondson.com/psychological-safety, accessed 5 November 2023

20   T Clark, *The 4 Stages of Psychological Safety: Defining the path to inclusion and innovation* (Berrett-Koehler Publishers, 2020)

21   T Sachs, 'Employee empowerment examples: Inspiring ways to empower your people' (HiBob blog, 26 September 2023), www.hibob.com/blog/employee-empowerment-examples, accessed 9 November 2023

22   T Sachs, 'Employee empowerment examples: Inspiring ways to empower your people'

(HiBob blog, 26 September 2023), www.hibob.
com/blog/employee-empowerment-examples,
accessed 9 November 2023

23 A Hall, 'Semco's radical transformation:
Embracing freedom and driving growth'
(AaronHall.com, 20 September 2023), https://
aaronhall.com/insights/semcos-radical-
transformation-embracing-freedom-and-driving-
growth, accessed 9 November 2023

24 T Sparkes, 'Why it is crucial to create leaders at
all levels', *Personnel Today* (12 September 2016),
www.personneltoday.com/hr/crucial-create-
leaders-levels, accessed 5 November 2016

25 W Craig, 'What businesses need in order to
develop a flat structure of leadership', *Forbes*
(6 February 2016), www.forbes.com/sites/
williamcraig/2018/02/06/what-businesses-
need-in-order-to-develop-a-flat-structure-
of-leadership/#a5c57d55d293, accessed 5
November 2023

26 A Groth, 'Zappos has quietly backed away from
holacracy', Quartz (29 January 2020), https://
qz.com/work/1776841/zappos-has-quietly-
backed-away-from-holacracy, accessed 20
December 2023

27 ProAptivity, 'The moment of truth' (nd), www.
proaptivity.com/a-moment-of-truth/, accessed
20 December 2023

28 J Wiles, 'The 5 pillars of successful strategy
execution' (Gartner, 17 July 2023), www.gartner.

com/smarterwithgartner/the-five-pillars-of-strategy-execution, accessed 4 November 2023

29 C Chavez and S Palsule, *Rehumanizing Leadership: Putting purpose back into business* (LID, 2020)

30 Akṣapāda, *1400 Lessons from the 14th Dalai Lama* (Google Books, nd), https://play.google.com/store/books/details/1400_LESSONS_FROM_THE_14TH_DALAI_LAMA?id=V_cqEAAAQBAJ&hl=en_US&gl=US&pli=1, accessed 5 November 2023

31 M Cheong, SM Spain, FJ Yammarino and S Yun, 'Two faces of empowering leadership: Enabling and burdening', *The Leadership Quarterly*, 27 (2016), 602–616, https://doi.org/10.1016/j.leaqua.2016.01.006

32 M Cheong, SM Spain, FJ Yammarino and S Yun, 'Two faces of empowering leadership: Enabling and burdening', *The Leadership Quarterly*, 27 (2016), 602–616, https://doi.org/10.1016/j.leaqua.2016.01.006

33 M Krakowsky, 'Empower employees to make things happen' (SHRM, 16 February 2019), www.shrm.org/hr-today/news/all-things-work/pages/empower-employees-to-make-things-happen.aspx, accessed 5 November 2023

34 I Hutchinson, *People Glue, Employee Engagement and Retention Solutions that Stick* (Warriewood, 2009)

35 D Conant, 'About Doug Conant' (Conant Leadership, nd), https://conantleadership.com/

about/doug-conant, accessed 5 November 5, 2023

36   Hubble, 'The official list of every company's back-to-office strategy' (Hubble, 8 September 2023), https://hubblehq.com/blog/famous-companies-workplace-strategies, accessed 5 November 2023

37   Telstra, 'The APAC Transformation Vision: Optimising for hybrid' (2022), www.telstra.com.sg/en/news-research/research/the-apac-transformation-vision-optimising-for-hybrid, accessed 5 November 2023

38   K Kuener-Hebert, 'How hybrid work can empower employees' (StrategicChro260, nd), https://strategicchro360.com/how-hybrid-work-can-empower-employees, accessed 5 November 2023

39   P Kuenkel, *The Art of Leading Collectively: Co-creating a sustainable, socially just future* (Chelsea Green, 2016)

Acknowledgments

I published the first edition of this book in 2021 to fill an obvious gap in the leadership and management published canon. Three years later, I am proud to call *Unleash the Inner CEO: Make distributed leadership a reality* a multi-award-winning, number-one international bestseller. I am so grateful to supporters, readers and reviewers around the world for its reception, and to my clients who have adopted my principles, models and tools to unleash the power of the many in their organizations.

As ever, there are so many people to thank for getting both the first and second editions out there. First off, a massive thanks to one-time customer, colleague, friend and now mentor, Greg McKibbin. Over dozens of catch-ups across Singapore and Melbourne, Greg helped me thrash out the original concept and, in true

Aussie style, did not let me get away with waffle, ill-considered ideas or doubt when hitting roadblocks. I am so grateful for his continuing, strong support.

Huge thanks also to my original book coaches who supported me through the process. First and foremost is Rachel Henke, whom I'd recommend to anyone thinking about getting their first business book from idea to reality. Alongside Rachel was Russell Cooper, whose advice around flow, sense and messaging was always on the money.

For the second edition and since the launch in 2021, I'd like to thank the incomparable Rebecca Duffy, book coach, devil's advocate, challenger and supporter, with a great eye for detail. I simply wouldn't have launched the second edition until the 2030s without Rebecca, I'm sure of it. Becs, you are an absolute star.

I'd also like to thank long-time collaborator Mohamed Khalid Maideen for his excellent design work, bringing to life the models in the book and their evolutions for the second edition.

Seven people provided the glue between the chapters in my book: my expert interviewees, whose passion for the subject matter and practical action in their own businesses to make leadership without levels actually happen, has provided readers with workable ideas, must-dos, "watch-outs" and best practices. Big thanks to Johanna Bolin Tingvall, at Spotify; Philippe Bonnet, formerly of Essilor; Steen Puggaard, co-founder of the phenomenal 4Fingers Crispy Chicken; Natasha Prasad, from Mambu; Emma Saxby, talent and HR expert and coach; and the wonderful Andrea Studlik, formerly of JLL. I'd also like to thank James Cross for providing an insightful look into how the armed forces empower troops at all levels and locations, and how "mission command" enables the whole thing to work. Big lessons for small, medium and large organizations. For this second edition, a further thanks to my empowered voices: Ehecatl Hunt-Duarte, Milvio DiBartolomeo and Rasie Bamigbade.

Finally, many thanks to Tim Lupinacci, CEO of Baker Donelson and founder of the social enterprise, "Everybody Leads", for his valuable insights as a champion of leaders without levels.

Thanks to all those who have been sounding boards for the idea and journey from the beginning – notably my former teammates in Singapore, including Belinda Ng, Antonio Codinach, Minh Thuy Phi, Rosalind Loh, Parima Jasina and Sandy Hernandez. Big respect!

A big shout out to those who have supported the journey through the first and into this second edition, and who have been cheerleaders for The Inner CEO among my clients: Joanne Flinn, Binu Bilan, Mette Johannsen, Don Rapley, Paul Marks, Robin Speculand, Georgia Ronald, Paul Hargreaves, Bruna Fontes, Jennifer Gillespie, Theresa Cheng, the folks at HP Inc, Xylem Inc, International SOS (big thanks to Michael Gardner for his support over the years), Univercells, Kevin Cottam, Dr Rochelle Haynes, MindDojo, EGN, Speexx, ILM, Forbes, Google Asia Pacific HQ, DSM-Firmenich, Harvard Business Review, Medium Online and so many more.

Last but not least, a big thanks to Steve Ashcroft, my first-ever line manager when I joined Procter & Gamble in 1990. Even then, Steve epitomized the spirit of this book, empowering, supporting and inspiring those who worked with and for him.

My sincerest apologies to anyone I have inadvertently missed, so many people have been there for me and I thank you all for it.

Finally, a big thank you to my awesome family – Jackie, Holly and Alex, who have all unleashed their inner CEO, it seems!

The Author

Jeremy is the multi award-winning Chief Executive of Performance Works International (PWI), co-founder of the social enterprise DiversITy-talent, and a Non-Executive Board Director for three other organizations.

Performance Works is a modern leadership research, consulting, and development company that helps organizations, executive boards, and leaders succeed in the digital climate amidst disruption, opportunity, and uncertainty. Jeremy's efforts in this area have been recently recognized by *The Independent newspaper*, UK, and their sister publication, *Business Reporter*, as winner of the "Best of Global

Business 2023" Award for the work he and his company deliver on the international stage.

Jeremy combines business and digital transformation expertise, leadership knowledge, and commercial success as an international CEO and executive board officer in the UK and Asia, with his experience as a corporate learning and human capital professional of over 25 years.

In parallel, Jeremy produces and hosts his own multi-platform "Rethink Leadership" podcast since 2020, which is now one of the top 1.5% of podcasts globally, bringing new leadership and transformation next practices from global experts to audiences everywhere.

As the global expert on empowered working, Jeremy is passionate about making distributed leadership the reality that has been promised for decades.

Find out more about Jeremy's programs at:

🌐 https://performanceworks.global/theinnerceo

Connect with Jeremy personally on social media at:

🛑 www.facebook.com/jeremy.blain.35

🔲 www.linkedin.com/in/jeremyblain

🔲 www.instagram.com/jeremyb01/